T0301813

FIXED REVENUE ACCOUNTING

A New Management Accounting Framework

Japanese Management and International Studies
(ISSN: 2010-4448)

Editor-in-Chief: Yasuhiro Monden *(University of Tsukuba, Japan)*

Published

Vol. 15   *Fixed Revenue Accounting: A New Management Accounting Framework*
edited by Kenichi Suzuki & Bruce Gurd

Vol. 14   *Holistic Business Process Management: Theory and Practice*
edited by Gunyung Lee, Masanobu Kosuga & Yoshiyuki Nagasaka

Vol. 13   *Management of Innovation Strategy in Japanese Companies*
edited by Kazuki Hamada & Shufuku Hiraoka

Vol. 12   *Lean Management of Global Supply Chain*
edited by Yasuhiro Monden & Yoshiteru Minagawa

Vol. 11   *Entrepreneurship in Asia: Social Enterprise, Network and Grassroots
Case Studies*
edited by Stephen Dun-Hou Tsai, Ted Yu-Chung Liu, Jersan Hu &
Shang-Jen Li

Vol. 10   *Management of Enterprise Crises in Japan*
edited by Yasuhiro Monden

Vol. 9   *Management of Service Businesses in Japan*
edited by Yasuhiro Monden, Noriyuki Imai, Takami Matsuo &
Naoya Yamaguchi

Vol. 8   *Management of an Inter-Firm Network*
edited by Yasuhiro Monden

Vol. 7   *Business Group Management in Japan*
edited by Kazuki Hamada

Vol. 6   *M&A for Value Creation in Japan*
edited by Yasuyoshi Kurokawa

Vol. 5   *Business Process Management of Japanese and Korean Companies*
edited by Gunyung Lee, Masanobu Kosuga, Yoshiyuki Nagasaka &
Byungkyu Sohn

Vol. 4   *International Management Accounting in Japan:
Current Status of Electronics Companies*
edited by Kanji Miyamoto

For the complete list of titles in this series, please go to
http://www.worldscientific.com/series/jmis

Japanese Management and International Studies – Vol. 15

FIXED REVENUE ACCOUNTING

A New Management Accounting Framework

editors

Kenichi Suzuki

Meiji University, Japan

Bruce Gurd

University of South Australia, Australia

World Scientific

NEW JERSEY · LONDON · SINGAPORE · BEIJING · SHANGHAI · HONG KONG · TAIPEI · CHENNAI · TOKYO

Published by

World Scientific Publishing Co. Pte. Ltd.

5 Toh Tuck Link, Singapore 596224

USA office: 27 Warren Street, Suite 401-402, Hackensack, NJ 07601

UK office: 57 Shelton Street, Covent Garden, London WC2H 9HE

Library of Congress Cataloging-in-Publication Data

Names: Suzuki, Kenichi, 1960 August 9–   editor. | Gurd, Bruce, 1956 September 3–   editor.
Title: Fixed revenue accounting : a new management accounting framework /
    edited by Kenichi Suzuki and Bruce Gurd.
Description: New Jersey : World Scientific, [2019] | Series: Japanese
    management and international studies (JMIS), ISSN 2010-4448 ; Vol 15
Identifiers: LCCN 2018012515 | ISBN 9789813237254
Subjects: LCSH: Revenue--Accounting.
Classification: LCC HF5681.R5 F59 2019 | DDC 657/.72--dc23
LC record available at https://lccn.loc.gov/2018012515

British Library Cataloguing-in-Publication Data

A catalogue record for this book is available from the British Library.

For any available supplementary material, please visit
https://www.worldscientific.com/worldscibooks/10.1142/10910#t=suppl

Desk Editor: Lum Pui Yee

Typeset by Stallion Press
Email: enquiries@stallionpress.com

Printed in Singapore

Japan Society of Organization and Accounting (JSOA)

Henry Aigbedo, Oakland University, USA
Mahmuda Akter, University of Dhaka, Bangladesh
Chao Hsiung Lee, National Chung Hsing University, Taiwan

Founder &Editor-in-Chief
Japanese Management and International Studies
Yasuhiro Monden, University of Tsukuba, Japan

Auditor
Takeshi Ito, Value Co-Creation, Inc., Tokyo, Japan

Assistant Managers
Satoshi Arimoto, Niigata university, Japan
Hiromasa Hirai, Kanagawa University, Japan

Mission of JSOA and Editorial Information

For the purpose of making a contribution to the business and academic communities, the Japan Society of Organization and Accounting (JSOA), is committed to publishing **Japanese Management and International Studies (JMIS), which is a refereed annual publication with a specific theme for each volume.**

The series is designed to inform the world about research outcomes of the new "Japanese-style management system" developed in Japan. However, as the series title suggests, it also promotes "*International Studies*" on the managerial competencies of various countries that include Asian countries as well as Western countries under the globalized business activities.   Research topics included in this series are management of organizations in a broad sense (including the business group or inter-firm network) and the accounting for managing the organizations. More specifically, topics include business strategy, business models, organizational restoration, corporate finance, M&A, environmental management, operations management, managerial & financial accounting, manager performance evaluation, reward systems. The research approach is interdisciplinary, which includes case studies, theoretical studies, normative studies and empirical studies, but emphasizes real world business.

Our JSOA's board of directors has established an editorial board of international standing. In each volume, guest editors who are experts on the volume's special theme serve as the volume editors. The details of JSOA is shown in its by-laws contained in the home-page: http://jsoa.sakura.ne.jp/english/index.html

Japanese Management
and International Studies (JMIS)

Preface

After the collapse of the bubble economy in Japan, we saw a miserable situation: The situation of frequent corporate bankruptcies, where many people lost their jobs or were anxious about losing their jobs. As a result, their families no longer lived in peace. Can management accounting soften the blow of large economic fluctuations? This is the background of fixed revenue accounting (FRA): FRA encourages employees to acquire and retain fixed customers where the fixed customers provide protection against economic crisis.

FRA is a new management accounting framework to evaluate and manage the impacts of fixed customers on a company's financials. Fixed customers refer to frequent or regular customers who are expected to repeat their purchases. Compared with non-fixed customers, fixed customers provide several advantages for a company. Their repeated purchases lead to stability of revenue, which makes profits more stable. Also, their repeated purchases bring about larger amounts of revenue which improves profitability because with the increase of revenue, the costs involved in keeping a customer do not change. Furthermore, the profitability and stability of fixed customers can be used for decision-making to encourage investment for future growth. Recognizing the advantages of fixed customers, I propose the framework to assess and manage the impacts of fixed customers on a company's financials to improve its performance.

FRA involves the following steps: First, the revenue, cost, and profit are assigned to customer segments defined by the strength of purchasing repetition. The strength of purchasing repetition is measured by the total amount or total number of transactions of each customer. With this measurement, customers are placed into the customer segments. Also, the revenues obtained from the customers are totaled for each customer segment. After matching the revenues to costs, the profits are calculated for each customer segment. Based on these accounting figures, the impacts of fixed customers on a company's financials are assessed. The comparison of revenues, costs, and profits among the customer segments shows the impacts of the strength of purchasing repetition to profits (Table 1).

Table 1. The basic form of FRA profit and loss statement.

		Total	New customers	Non-fixed customers	Fixed customers	Defector
Sales (Revenue)	Product A					
	Product B					
	Product C					
	Sub total					
Traceable variable cost	Cost of goods sold					
	Selling expenses					
	Sub total					
Marginal profit					(a)	
Traceable fixed cost	Cost of goods sold					
	Selling expenses					
	Sub total	(b)				
Contribution margin						
Untraceable fixed cost	Cost of goods sold					
	Selling expenses					
	Sub total	(c)				
Operation profit						
Fixed operation profit			※ Fixed operation profit = (a) − (b) − (c)			

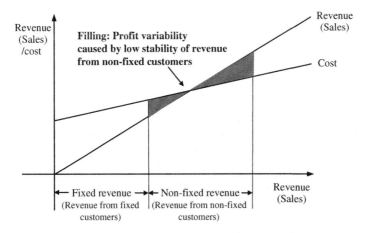

Fig. 1 Fixed customers and profit variability.

Also, the portion of revenue of the fixed customer segment in total revenues demonstrate a company's profit stability because revenue of the segment are more stable than those of other segments (Fig. 1).

In addition, with the comparison between budgeted and actual numbers, this demonstrates the impact of the difference of the strength in each customer segment. The next stage is where customer policy for improving the company's financials is established.

This book contains four parts. The first three parts introduce the benefits of adopting FRA in business. To help readers' understanding, these parts include theoretical explanations and case studies of Japanese manufacturing or service companies. The last part discusses some topics of management accounting in Japanese companies.

PART 1: Profitability Analysis

The profit and loss statement of FRA supports in helping to identify and manage profitability of fixed customers. Part 1 introduces two cases: A department store and a mail-order company in Japan identified the impact of fixed customers on profits by using FRA profit and loss statements and changed marketing strategy in order to help increase their profits by focusing on the fixed customers. Also, this part discusses a case where a Japanese hotel chain found key factors to satisfy fixed customers and increase revenue by analyzing the relationship between customer satisfaction and customer purchasing amounts, measured by a questionnaire survey.

PART 2: Stability Analysis

Part 2 demonstrates that a lot of fixed customers can increase and provide sustainability of revenue and profits. A case study of the hotel chain describes this proposition by using each customer's transaction data.

PART 3: Growth Analysis

The Bathtub Model (Fig. 2), one of the components of the FRA model, enhances the visibility of profit growth by showing customers' movement in the customer segments; new customers, fixed customers, non-fixed customers, and defectors.

Part 3 discusses three issues: First, Bathtub Model variance analysis which was developed by applying the bathtub model to variance analysis; second, the advantages of the bathtub model variance analysis against

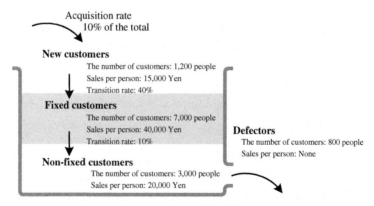

※ Only describes the main route from each segment to the next

Fig. 2   Bathtub Model conceptual framework.

conventional variance analysis with the semiconductor trading company/manufacturer case; and third, growth analysis utilizing the bathtub model variance analysis at the hotel chain.

PART 4: Related Topics in Management Accounting

Part 4 contains three topics of management accounting in Japanese companies.

Kenichi Suzuki
Department Chair, Professor
Department of Accounting
School of Business Administration
Meiji University
1 October, 2018

About the Editors

 **Dr. Kenichi Suzuki** is a professor of School of Business Administration and a chair of accounting department, Meiji University after he worked for Institute of The Long-Term Credit Bank of Japan (1984–1998) and Hiroshima International University (1998–2001). He is a deputy editor-in-chief of The Journal of Japanese Management Accounting and an editor-in-chief of Japanese Journal of Strategic Management.

He got a master in Business Administration from Tsukuba University and a PhD in Economics from Osaka University, and also won the IMA Annual Lybrand Awards (1999–2000), The Japan Cost Accounting Association Awards (2000), and The Japan Management Accounting Association Awards (2014).

Now, he is (1) developing a framework of Fixed Revenue Accounting, a new management accounting system to encourage employees to have customer-oriented perspectives, (2) examining the importance of communication in management control process based on the theory of 'Ba' which refers to a mechanism to explain how employees are motivated to work together and (3) investigating a MCS package consisted of budgeting and hoshin-kanri system.

Dr. Bruce Gurd is an Associate Professor in the School of Management at the University of South Australia and a Deputy Director of the Australian Centre for Asian Business. The focus of his research has been organizational performance management systems including the measurement of social impact.

He graduated with a PhD from the University of Adelaide in management control systems. More recently he has been researching more broadly in strategy and has completed a book on Strategy Execution in complex environments. He has taught in the MBA at the University of South Australia for nearly 20 years in strategy, management and accounting for managers.

He was recognised as a Life Fellow of the Australia and New Zealand Academy of Management.

Contents

List of Contributors

Bruce Gurd
Associate Professor,
School of Management,
University of South Australia
GPO Box 2471 Adelaide,
South Australia, 5000, Australia
bruce.gurd@unisa.edu.au

John Hatzinikolakis
Lecturer, School of Management,
University of South Australia
GPO Box 2471, Adelaide,
South Australia, 5001, Australia
John.Hatzinikolakis@unisa.edu.au

Masahiro Hosoda
Lecturer, College of Humanities
and Social Sciences, Ibaraki University
2-1-1 Bunkyo, Mito,
Ibaraki, 310-8512, Japan
masahiro.hosoda.mn@vc.ibaraki.ac.jp

Yu Hiasa
Postgraduate, Graduate School of
Business Administration, Meiji University,
Research Fellow of the Japan Society
for the Promotion of Science
1-1 Kanda-Surugadai, Chiyoda-ku,
Tokyo, 101-8301, Japan
hiasa@ken-suzuki.net

Yuki Iwabuchi
iRidge, Inc.
1-11-9 BPRpureisu kamiyatyou
9F/10F, Azabudai, Minato-ku,
Tokyo, 106-0041, Japan
yuuki.iwbuchi0109@ken-suzuki.net

Shuhei Kawata
Senior Manager, iRidge, Inc., Postgraduate,
Graduate School of Business Administration, Meiji University
1-1 Kanda-Surugadai, Chiyoda-ku,
Tokyo, 101-8301, Japan
shkawata@ken-suzuki.net

Maiko Kodama
Postgraduate, Graduate School of
Business Administration, Meiji University
1-1 Kanda-Surugadai, Chiyoda-ku,
Tokyo, 101-8301, Japan
kodama@ken-suzuki.net

Misa Kikyo
Postgraduate, Graduate School of
Business Administration, Meiji University
1-1 Kanda-Surugadai, Chiyoda-ku,
Tokyo, 101-8301, Japan
kikyo@ken-suzuki.net

Ayuko Komura
Postgraduate, Graduate School of
Business Administration, Meiji University,
Research Fellow of the Japan Society
for the Promotion of Science
1-1 Kanda-Surugadai, Chiyoda-ku,
Tokyo, 101-8301, Japan
kom-ayu@ken-suzuki.net

Kohsuke Matsuoka
Associate Professor, Faculty of
Business Administration,
Tohoku Gakuin University
1-3-1 Tsuchitoi, Aoba-ku, Sendai,
Miyagi, 980-8511, Japan
matsuoka@mail.tohoku-gakuin.ac.jp

Kayo Mitani
Postgraduate, Graduate School of
Business Administration, Meiji University,
Research Fellow of the Japan Society
for the Promotion of Science
1-1 Kanda-Surugadai, Chiyoda-ku,
Tokyo, 101-8301, Japan
hug.u.x@ken-suzuki.net

Kazuyoshi Morimoto
Professor, Faculty of Social Sciences,
Hagoromo University of International Studies
1-89-1 Hamaderaminami, Nishi-ku, Sakai,
Osaka, 592-8344, Japan
kmorimoto@hagoromo.ac.jp

Yoshitaka Myochin
Postgraduate, Graduate School of
Business Administration, Meiji University
1-1 Kanda-Surugadai, Chiyoda-ku,
Tokyo, 101-8301, Japan
myochin@ken-suzuki.net

Masanobu Nakamura
Associate Professor, Graduate School of
Management, Kagawa University
1-1 Saiwaicho, Takamatsu,
Kagawa, 760-8521, Japan
msnakamura@gsm.kagawa-u.ac.jp

Takeshi Saito
Lecturer, School of Management,
Chukyo University
101-2 Yagoto Honmachi, Showa-ku,
Nagoya, Aichi, 466-8666, Japan
saitou@ken-suzuki.net

Kenichi Suzuki
Professor, Chair of Accounting Department
School of Business Administration
Meiji University
1-1 Kanda-Surugadai, Chiyoda-ku,
Tokyo, 101-8301, Japan
kgh00111@ken-suzuki.net

Daisuke Tomita
Certified Public Accountant, Ministry of
Health, Labor and Welfare
1-2-2 Kasumigaseki, Chiyoda-ku,
Tokyo, 100-8916 Japan
tomita-daisuke99@mhlw.go.jp

Hitomi Toyosaki
Postgraduate, Graduate School of
Business Administration, Meiji University,
Research Fellow of the Japan Society
for the Promotion of Science
1-1 Kanda-Surugadai, Chiyoda-ku,
Tokyo, 101-8301, Japan
toyosaki@ken-suzuki.net

Kaori Yamawaki
Assistant professor, School of
Management, Shukutoku University
1150-1, Fujikubo, Miyoshi, Iruma,
Saitama, 354-8510, Japan
yamawaki@ken-suzuki.net

Part 1
Profitability Analysis

Chapter 1

Profitability of Fixed Customers: A Case of a Japanese Department Store

Kenichi Suzuki, Misa Kikyo, Maiko Kodama,
Hitomi Toyosaki, Yu Hiasa, and Kohsuke Matsuoka

1. Introduction

Fixed revenue accounting (FRA) was developed by the first author as a new management accounting framework to evaluate the impacts of fixed customers on a company's financials (Suzuki, 2005; Asada *et al.*, 2005). Fixed customers refer to frequent or regular customers who are expected to repeat their purchases. Compared with non-fixed customers, fixed customers produce several advantages for a company. Their repeat purchases introduce some stability in revenue, which also leads to some stability in profit. In addition, their repeat purchases bring in a large amount of revenue that improves a company's profitability because with the increase of revenue, the cost to keep a customer does not change. Recognizing these advantages of having fixed customers, we propose a framework to assess the impacts of fixed customers on a company's financials to improve its performance.

To evaluate the impacts, FRA requires the following steps: First, the strength of repeat purchases is measured by the total number or total amount of transactions for each customer. Based on this measurement, each customer is placed into the fixed or non-fixed customer segment. Next, the revenues obtained from the customers are totaled for each customer segment. Also, after matching the revenues to costs, the profits are calculated for each customer segment. Based on these accounting figures, the impacts of the fixed customers on a company's financials are assessed. Comparing revenues, costs, and profits across the customer segments reveals the impacts of the fixed customers. Furthermore, the comparison between budgeted and actual figures shows how the company's customer strategy can be refined.

The strength of FRA is in the ability to identify the stability of revenue and profit as well as the profitability for frequent customers. Development of a management accounting framework to identify the stability and the profitability obtained from frequent customers began with the responses to two questions that the first author asked himself in 2001. From the concepts of fixed and variable costs, the first question occurred: "Why isn't revenue classified into fixed and variable categories?" Adapting the concept of income momentum, which was defined by Ijiri (1990), as an expected income in consecutive periods assuming no environmental change, the FRA approach for classifying revenue into stable and not stable categories was developed. Relationship marketing which insists that a company can improve its profitability by increasing its frequent customers led to the other question: "How are the impacts of frequent customers on financials measured?" Referring to customer profitability analyses proposed by Foster and Gupta (1994), Foster *et al.* (1996) and Foster and Young (1997), the FRA approach for identifying the profitability for frequent customers was established.

In management accounting, a framework focusing on the evaluation for the impacts of fixed customers does not exist. What does exist is studies on management accounting, which can be grouped into two categories: the effectiveness of non-financial measurements from the customer perspective, and the analyses of customer profitability. Kaplan and Norton (1996) stated the necessity of non-financial measurements from the customer perspective. To examine the effectiveness for the non-financial measurement, Ittner and Larcker (1998), Banker *et al.* (2000), and Smith and Wright (2004) tested the correlation between the customer satisfaction index and companies' financials, and Hemmer (1996) and Smith (2002) investigated the usefulness of the index based on mathematical models. These studies indicate the effectiveness of non-financial measurements from the customer perspective but had no intention to develop a framework for evaluating the impacts of customers based on financial figures. On the other hand, Foster and Gupta (1994), Foster *et al.* (1996), and Foster and Young (1997) discussed the framework for analyzing customer profitability by financial figures. Their framework presented valuable insights such as the usefulness of transaction data based on each customer and profit estimations for an extended period of time to understand the customer profitability. However, this framework did not focus on evaluating frequent customers.

The purpose of this chapter is to make the case to demonstrate the strength of FRA which identifies the profitability related to frequent customers. We start this chapter by presenting three conditions for FRA. Next, we demonstrate and examine a profit and loss statement for FRA using a department store's case. Finally, conclusions are provided.

2. Three Requirements for Fixed Revenue Accounting

FRA can be undertaken when these three conditions exist: (1) customer segments must be categorized by the strength of repeat purchases of each customer, (2) the strength must be measured by the transaction data, and (3) the transaction data must be recorded for each customer.

2.1 *Customer segments categorized by the strength of repeat purchases of each customer*

FRA is accounting based on customer segments categorized by the Strength of Repeat Purchases of Each Customer in a certain period (SRPEC). Generally, to evaluate the impact of a driving factor on a company's financials, management accounting segments its financial results according to the driving factor. For example, to evaluate the impact of the customer's region on the financials, the financial results are divided by the regions. Then, by comparing the results, the regional impact is identified. This basic approach in management accounting is applied to FRA in order to evaluate the impact of the SRPEC.

By limiting the SRPEC with a range, customers can be segmented into two customer segments of: non-fixed Customers, with a low SRPEC and fixed customers, with a high SRPEC. In addition, when a company has classified the customers at two points in the time, it can identify their changes in the customer segments.

With this information, the customer segments of non-fixed customers with a low SRPEC and fixed customers with a high SRPEC can both be separated into two customer segments: non-fixed customers, with a low SRPEC in two consecutive periods, semi-fixed customers, with a low SRPEC in a last period but a high SRPEC in a period before the last one, fixed customers, with a high SRPEC in two consecutive periods, and semi-non-fixed customers, with a high SRPEC in a last period but a low SRPEC in a period before the last one.

2.2 The strength measured by transaction data

The SRPEC is measured by the transaction data. As a basic measurement for the SRPEC, the total amount, the total number, or consecutive periods of transactions is listed. When a company chooses the measurement from its transaction data, it must consider the relationship of the measurement for the SRPEC to its corporate value. The corporate value is regarded as the sum of discounted cash flows to be gained from customers during the years that they will continue to make transactions. The total amount of transactions becomes a measurement for the SRPEC because it affects each year's cash flow. Another measurement, the consecutive period of transactions, is selected because it influences the total value of the discounted cash flow. Finally, the total number of transactions is a powerful measurement because it can be reflected to the transactional momentum on the transactional amount and period.

Because many other measurements for the SRPEC will be developed in future business practice, let's look at the responses to the question: "When your company identifies customers with whom your company wants to establish strong relationships, what is the most desirable measurement?" In 2006, the first author asked this question to seven MBA students who were working for companies. "Measurement for identifying important customer relationship" in Table 1 shows how widely companies define the measurements for the SRPEC. However, these varied measurements for

Table 1.   The measurements for identifying the important customer relationship.

Type of business	Sales volume (million USD)	Major customers	Measurement for identifying important customer relationship	Categories of measurements			
				Amount	Period	Number	Others
Consumable items wholesale	17	Hotels	More than continual 10 thousands USD sales per month from major 5 items for 5 consecutive years	✓	✓	—	—
Foods wholesale	15	Retailers	Credit selling approval based on the number, the value and the consective poriod of sales	✓	✓	✓	—
Temporary employment agency	2	Small companies	Decision by president	—	—	—	✓
Business application software developer	83	Accounting departments	Continual sales years	—	✓	—	—
Apparel manufacturer	333	Retailers	Decision by regional sales manager	—	—	—	✓
Treatment Device manufacturer	4.2	Parts manufacturer	More than 9 times transaction per year	—	—	✓	—
Auto parts manufacturer	600	Auto parts manufacturer	More than 83 millions USD sales for 3 consecutive years	✓	✓	—	—
Pharmaceutical manufacturer	1,667	Hospitals	More than 5 consecutive years' sales	—	✓	—	—

seven companies can be identified as one of the three basic measurements described in the prior paragraph, the total amount, the total number or consecutive period of transactions. See "Categories of measurements" in Table 1 and remember that this result cannot be generalized because the samples were not selected at random.

2.3 *The transaction data recorded for each customer*

To measure the SRPEC, the transaction data must be recorded for each customer. Transactions should be recorded with each customer's identification such as the name, enabling a company to identify to which customer segment each customer belongs to.

Consider the possibility of recording the customer identification with each transaction in two types of commerce: business to business and business to consumers. In business to business commerce, the customer identification is usually attached to each transaction record, while in business to consumer commerce, it depends on the industry. Many industries, such as for example, airlines, hotels, hospitals, communications, and mail-order, require the customer to register and thus store the transaction records by name. Other industries such as retail and restaurants don't customarily ask for any customer registration and have anonymous transaction records; but they can collect the transactions of important customers as named records, by using frequency or loyalty programs. Additionally, the spread of electronic settlements on a company credit card or the wallet-cell phone is making it easier for the company to introduce frequency or loyalty programs.

2.4 *Profit and loss framework in fixed revenue accounting*

By matching costs with the revenues calculated according to the four customer segments, non-fixed, semi-non-fixed, fixed, and semi-fixed, a basic form of profit and loss statements for the customer relationship evaluation can be produced (as shown in Table 2). Note that this statement supposes that costs are categorized into traceable and untraceable costs to the customer segment and into variable and fixed costs based on a cost driver, the sales amount.

Table 2.   The basic form of profit and loss statements based on Suzuki (2007, p. 219).

		Total	Friend (non-fixed)	Sweetheart (semi-fixed)	Family (fixed)	Ex-family (semi-non-fixed)
Sales (Revenue)	Product A					
	Product B					
	Product C					
	Sub total					
Traceable variable cost	Cost of goods sold					
	Selling expenses					
	Sub total	(b)				
Marginal profit						
Traceable fixed cost	Cost of goods sold					
	Selling expenses					
	Sub total					
Contribution margin						
Untraceable fixed cost	Cost of goods sold					
	Selling expenses					
	Sub total	(c)			(a)	
Operation profit						
	Fixed operation profit					

What percentage of the total revenue is made up by fixed customers?
Does a company offer an assortment of goods which satisfies fixed customers' requirements?
Is the assortment profitable?

Were sales activities efficient?

Is the profitability of fixed customers high?

※ Fixed operation profit = (a) – (b) – (c)

Note that the fixed operating profit, calculated by subtracting the fixed costs from the marginal profit obtained from the fixed customer, evaluated the offset between the revenue and the fixed costs. The meaning of the fixed operating income is described in Part 3.

3. The Department Store's Case Study

3.1 *The department store's motivation of using the profit and loss concept*

As a pioneer of a loyalty program in Japan, the department store (DS) maintained a loyalty program that gives members a price reduction benefit of either 5% or 10% on current purchases depending on the total value of their purchases in previous years. However, experiencing the low growth in profit during the Japanese economic recession, the managers of the DS began to argue for or against the 10% price reduction rate. The head of the sales division argued for applying the higher reduction rate in order to keep their loyal members, while the head of the buying division insisted that the 10% discount rate had a negative impact on the profit. During this conflict, the DS introduced the profit and loss concept of the FRA to financially evaluate the effects of the rates (Suzuki, 2007).

3.2 *The department store's customer segments and profit and loss statements*

The DS categorized the members of the loyalty program based on their price discount rates for the two years, 2010 and 2011, and into four types: "Friend" meaning the non-fixed customer, "Sweetheart" meaning the semi-fixed customer, "Family" meaning the fixed customer, and "Ex-family" meaning the semi-non-fixed customer (see Table 3).

Based on the four customer segments, the DS developed profit and loss statements to measure the contribution margin for each store. Table 4 shows the profit and loss statement and the reference data of Store A as an example. Please note these three facts: The price discount rates did not apply to some branded merchandises, such as Chanel products, but sometimes exceeded the regular discount rates offered in a New Year's sale, for example. The sales departments of the DS are basically organized by

Table 3.   The DS's customer segments.

		The price reduction rate in 2011	
		5%	10%
The price reduction rate in 2010	5%	Friend (non-fixed customer)	Sweetheart (semi-fixed customer)
	10%	Ex-family (semi-non-fixed customer)	Family (fixed customer)

type of merchandise. The figures in this statement were produced by multiplying the actual number by a certain number in order to maintain some confidentiality.

3.3 The department store's findings and decisions

The trends shown in sample Fig. 4 hold for all of the DS' stores. The family segment, the segment of fixed customers, made up a significant share of the contribution margin. On average, while 32% of all members, the family segment accounted for a contribution margin of 80%. Also, although the family segment consisted of the customers who enjoyed the highest discount rate of 9.7%, the family segment had the highest profitability. Averaged company wide, when compared with the friend segment, the family segment outperformed the friend segment in its ratio of contribution margin to sales by five points.

These two powerful results in the family segment are explained by the considerably large sum of sales divided over its traceable fixed cost. Referring back to Table 3, we find that the multiple of sales to traceable fixed cost is: 11 times in the friend segment, 69 times in the sweetheart segment, 137 times in the family segment, and 21 times in the ex-family segment.

The large profit share and high profitability of the family segment settled the arguments about the 10% price discount rate and encouraged the DS to expand the privileges. The DS expanded free parking benefits and added delivery services for the family segment. In addition, a discount rate over 10% is being considered for the members whose total value of purchases in two consecutive years has been above a certain large amount.

Table 4. Store A's profit and loss statement and data.

Store A 4/1/2010-3/31/2011 (000.Yen)		Total	Friend (non-fixed)	Sweetheart (semi-fixed)	Family (fixed)	Ex-family (semi-non-fixed)
Sales	Floor A	304,000	15,000	17,000	227,000	45,000
	Floor B	897,000	52,000	60,000	640,000	145,000
	—	—	—	—	—	—
	Sub total	5,299,000	503,000	480,000	4,110,000	206,000
Variable cost	Cost of goods sold	3,179,000	312,000	298,000	2,442,000	127,000
	Discount for members	465,000	20,000	34,000	397,000	14,000
	Sub total	3,644,000	332,000	332,000	2,839,000	141,000
	Marginal profit	1,655,000	171,000	148,000	1,271,000	65,000
Traceable fixed cost	Direct mail cost	19,000	10,000	1,000	6,000	2,000
	Services for members	75,000	37,000	6,000	24,000	8,000
	Sub total	94,000	47,000	7,000	30,000	10,000
	Contribution margin	1,561,000	124,000	141,000	1,241,000	55,000

Reference data		Total	Friend (non-fixed)	Sweetheart (semi-fixed)	Family (fixed)	Ex-family (semi-non-fixed)
Distribution ratio	Sales	100%	9%	9%	78%	4%
	Marginal profit	100%	10%	9%	77%	4%
	Contribution margin	100%	8%	9%	80%	4%
Margin ratio	Marginal profit	31%	34%	31%	31%	32%
	Contribution margin	29%	25%	29%	30%	27%
Price discount ratio		8.8%	4.0%	7.1%	9.7%	6.8%
Multiple of sales to traceable fixed cost		56	11	69	137	21
Members	Number	151,000	72,000	13,000	48,000	18,000
	Distribution ratio	100%	48%	9%	32%	12%
Per member	Sales	35,093	6,986	36,923	85,625	11,444
	Marginal profit	10,960	2,375	11,385	26,479	3,611
	Contribution margin	10,338	1,722	10,846	25,854	3,056

3.4 *Future scope of FRA study*

During this case study, we were able to establish two new researches for FRA to answer the questions raised by the DS, which are explained, respectively, in Sections 3.4.1 and 3.4.2.

3.4.1 *Bathtub Model*

The DS raised two questions: how changes in customers' SRPEC affect marginal profit and whether or not profit and loss statements in FRA can help them identify drivers to convert a new customer into a fixed customer. To answer the first question, we reorganized the previous four customer segments. Family and Sweetheart are integrated into fixed customer; friends and ex-family into non-fixed customer; and two new segments, namely, new customer and defector are added. After collecting data for those segments, we implemented a Bathtub Model, an accounting model specific to FRA (see Fig. 1).

The Bathtub Model is a model to demonstrate how the number of customers fluctuates according to customer acquisition rate or defection rate, and how customer composition changes with transition rate between

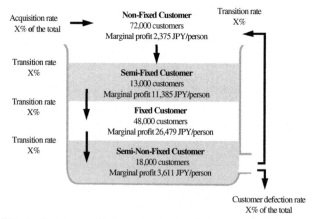

Fig. 1 Bathtub model in DS.

customer segments. The Bathtub Model-based analysis in this case clarified that effective strategies for achieving the DS's medium-term profit targets are to improve their customer acquisition rate and transition rate from new customers to fixed ones, while lowering transition rate from fixed ones to non-fixed.

The results of the analysis suggest that the Bathtub Model is a useful method for growth potential analysis. More precisely, it enables us to predict future customer numbers and analyze growth potential of marginal profit by multiplying the predicted number by marginal profit per customer. The Bathtub Model was originally referred to as "A Bathtub Model" because customer demographics, in other words, correlation between changes in the number of customers and those in the customer composition, is analogous to the hot water circulating mechanism for a bathtub. For more details about the Bathtub Model, please see Part 3.

3.4.2 *Variance analysis framework in FRA: VAF*

The second question was about whether or not profit and loss statements in FRA could help the DS identify drivers to convert a new customer into a repeat customer. To answer the question, we developed a specific variance analysis framework for FRA (FRA:VAF) to explore the driving factors. In VAF, we broke the contribution margin variance into the number of customer variance and the purchase amount variance per customer. The results of those variance analyses indicate that a majority of favorable contribution margin variances is attributed to favorable purchase amount variances.

In addition, we broke favorable purchase amount variances down into the number of floor variance, the purchase amount variance per floor. The results of the analyses demonstrate that a majority of favorable purchase amount variance is attributed to variance of the number of floor (see Fig. 2).

Consequently, we strongly recognized that encouraging customers' shop-around behavior is a key driver to acquire more fixed customers. Then, we started to apply contribution margin variance analysis extensively to customers by age group in order to develop innovative floors for encouraging their shop-around behavior and figure out effective ways of communication to notify customers of it.

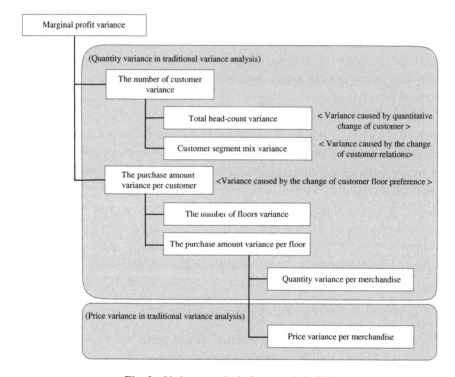

Fig. 2   Variance analysis framework in DS.

A key feature of FRA:VAF developed in this study is to analyze traditional quantity variances with perspectives of customer relationship such as changes in the number of customers, customer quality, product preference and purchase quantity, and therefore, FRA:VAF, compared with traditional variance analysis, has great potential to lead to more concrete decision-making in marketing.

For details about FRA:VAF, please refer to Part 4.

4. Conclusion

By using the DS case, this study aims to demonstrate the strength of FRA which identifies the profitability for fixed customers. The DS's case demonstrated the high effectiveness of FRA profit and loss concept on decision-making about customer relationship policies. The profit and loss statement in FRA clarified the powerful potentiality of the family segment, settled the arguments about the price discount rate, and encouraged the DS to expand the privileges of its loyalty program.

The study also revealed three limitations for getting benefits from the profit and loss statement concept. The first is, the greater part of profits must be gained from fixed customers in order to evaluate the impact of the strength of the customer relationship on the profitability. The second is, there should be a number of customers to collect adequate data. FRA needs enough number of customers to be segmented along transaction continuity for measuring such segments as accounting information, as we did in the study. Otherwise, it is difficult to grasp how much influence transaction continuity has over financial performance by using FRA.

The third is, transaction continuity must be an important factor for financial performance of a company wishing to use FRA. We consider that FRA might work less effectively for a company if a large portion of its revenue and profits, unlike in case of DS, are not earned by small number of fixed customers.

Finally, the study brought us new research ideas concerning Bathtub Model and FRA: VAF. Further studies on them will need to be performed.

References

Asada, T., Yori, M., Suzuki, K., Nakagawa, Y., and Sasaki, I. 2005. *Introduction to Management Accounting*, Tokyo: Yuhikaku Publishing Co., Ltd. (In Japanese).

Banker, R. D., Gordon, P., and Srinivasan, D. 2000. An Empirical Investigation of an Incentive Plan that Includes Nonfinancial Performance Measures, *The Accounting Review*, 75(1), 65–92.

Foster, G. and M. Gupta. 1994. Marketing, Cost Management and Management Accounting, *Journal of Management Accounting Research*, 6, 43–77.

Foster, G., Gupta, M., and Sjoblom, L. 1996. Customer Profitability Analysis: Challenges and New Directions, *Journal of Cost Management*, 10, 5–17.

Foster, G. and Young, S. M. 1997. Frontiers of Management Accounting Research, *Journal of Management Accounting Research*, 9, 63–77.

Hemmer, T. 1996. On the Design and Choice of "Modern" Management Accounting Measurers, *Journal of Management Accounting Research*, 8, 87–116.

Ijiri, Y. 1990. *Introduction to Momentum Accounting*, Tokyo: Nikkei Inc. (In Japanese).

Ittner, C. D. and Larcker, D. F. 1998. Are Nonfinancial Measures Leading Indicators of Financial Performance? An Analysis of Customer Satisfaction, *Journal of Accounting Research*, 36, 1–35.

Kaplan, R. S. and Norton, D. P. 1996. *The Balanced Scorecard: Translating Strategy into Action*. Boston, MA: Harvard Business School Press.

Matsuoka, K. and Suzuki, K. 2008. A Variance Analysis in Fixed Revenue Accounting: The Framework and a Case Study for Customer Relationship Variance Analysis, *The Journal of Cost Accounting Research*, 32(1), 85–97. (In Japanese).

Smith, M. J. 2002. Gaming Nonfinancial Performance Measures, *Journal of Management Accounting Research*, 14(1), 119–133.

Smith, R. E. and Wright, W. F. 2004. Determinants of Customer Loyalty and Financial Performance, *Journal of Management Accounting Research*, 16(1), 183–205.

Suzuki, K. 2005. An Evaluation Model of Profit Stability Based on the Concept of Fixed Revenue. *Bulletin of the Institute of Social Sciences, Meiji University*, 43(2), 163–174 (In Japanese).

Suzuki, K. 2007. A Consideration on the Applicability of Fixed Revenue Accounting. *The Accounting*, 171(2), 218–229 (In Japanese).

Suzuki, K. 2008. Current Situation and Problems of Fixed Revenue Accounting. *Meiji Business Review*, 55(4), 91–109 (In Japanese).

Chapter 2

Redesign and Management of Marketing Strategies Using FRA Profitability Analysis: A Case of a Mail-Order Company under Turnaround Process

Shuhei Kawata, John Hatzinikolakis, Takeshi Saito and Kaori Yamawaki

1. Introduction

1.1 *The purpose and significance of this study*

The purpose of this study is to examine the case of Company A, a mail-order company that uses fixed revenue accounting (FRA), to assist in determining whether quantifying the differences in profitability among customer segments is a useful tool for determining prioritization of resource allocation when considering marketing strategies.

FRA has been discussed in prior research conducted by its originators, in Suzuki (2007) and Matsuoka and Suzuki (2008, 2009), through case studies of the hotel industry and two retailers. These studies helped develop the concept of FRA, and explored whether it could be useful in determining types of business continuity issues. However, case studies on FRA have been conducted on only three companies to date. This study is significant in that it could serve to popularize FRA as a managerial accounting tool by exploring its effectiveness in contributing to marketing strategies through profitability analysis, which is one part of FRA, in the mail-order sector, which has not been examined in prior research.

In addition, we posit that mail-order companies need to be familiar with FRA and its usefulness as a management tool in computing promotion costs[1] for acquiring new customers based on customers' lifetime value[2] from their repeat purchases, especially if the initial transaction is unprofitable on a stand-alone basis, rather than looking at the profitability of each individual transaction.

2. Research Design

2.1 *Research method*

The method of this research is action research.

First, we introduce company A, which is the research-site of this study and explain the purpose of the introduction of FRA. Next, we explain three steps in the application of FRA to company A, which are as follows: (1) divide customers into four segments using the degree of customer relationships, (2) classify revenue and cost items by four customer segments, and (3) build profit and loss statements allocated by the four customer segments.

Analysis techniques related to FRA (see Figure 1), as introduced by Suzuki (2012, p. 80–81) include profitability analysis, growth analysis, difference analysis, stability analysis, revenue driver analysis, satisfaction index difference analysis, investment timing analysis, and allowable investment analysis. In this research, we focus on the profitability analysis and summarize suggestions for restructuring company A's marketing strategies.

2.2 *Description of research site (company A)*

Company A, the subject of this study, was founded in 2000 as a mail-order company marketing white coats, nurses' footwear, and medical equipment

---

[1] "Promotion costs" refers to the advertising and promotion costs and the marketing promotion costs involved in acquiring new customers.
[2] "Lifetime value" refers to the value to the firm from the total business from an individual customer from the initial to the final transaction, and not of each individual transaction by that customer.

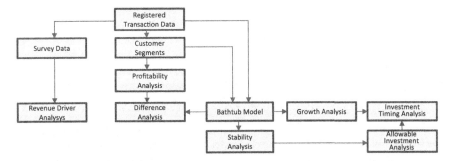

Fig. 1 Analytical relationships in FRA.

Source: Suzuki (2012, p. 81).

such as stethoscopes and sphygmomanometers to hospitals, clinics, and individual nurses through catalogs and on the internet.

Its target customers are a niche market consisting of individuals numbering about 1.45 million nurses and institutions numbering about 8,500 hospitals and 100,000 medical clinics. It has grown its business by direct marketing through catalog distribution. In addition, it tends to have long-term repeat business, as it regularly sends catalogs to customers who have ordered from the company in the past.

Company A has a client list of 180,000 customers, most of whom have made purchases in the past. These customers consist primarily of individual nurses and medical and nursing institutions such as hospitals, clinics, dental offices, and nursing facilities. Approximately three times a year, the company mails the customers on this list of about 150,000, 220-page catalogs containing some 5,000 SKUs[3] of about 1,000 items in various sizes and colors. Orders are received via fax, telephone, internet, and the postcards enclosed with the catalogs. The average order size is two to three items, while the average order amount is 6,000–7,000 JPY, and the average order frequency has been 1.5 times per year.

Under these market conditions, company A's sales had steadily grown since its inception, along with the expansion of the mail-order market to nurses. However, it was unable to achieve sufficient sales to cover the large marketing promotion costs involved in catalog production and

---

[3] "Stock keeping unit (SKU)" refers to the smallest inventory control units, which classify product varieties into such categories as size, color, version, etc.

distribution, and it had never recorded a profit since its founding. Furthermore, it was on the losing end of fierce competition with a rival company. Its annual sales peaked in 2007, then fell by about 40% over the three years from 2008 to 2010 (from 840 million JPY to 510 million JPY).

Due to these circumstances, in September 2011, company A was acquired by company B, and listed on the first section of the Tokyo Stock Exchange, and where one of the authors (Kawata) was employed. However, in its final year of operation before being acquired (October 2010–September 2011), it recorded sales of about 550 million JPY, and an operating loss of 67 million JPY. If it was to survive, it needed to take quick action to turnaround its sales and improve profitability.

2.3 Why company A introduced FRA

In rebuilding company A's business, we looked for a framework that would provide a way for the company to reorganize by acquiring a highly precise quantitative understanding of the basic reasons contributing to its poor performance.

Through pre-acquisition due diligence, we projected that one of the major reasons for the poor performance was degradation of the customer list due to insufficient efforts to develop repeat customers. However, it was not possible to measure this quantitatively because no appropriate method of doing so existed and because there was no employee placed to perform such an analysis.

To link customer relations with financial performance, we adopted FRA, creating an income statement for each customer segment based on the customer-relationship category. This enabled us to ascertain a quantitative understanding of the basic factors in the company's poor performance and enabled us to proceed with exploring ways to rebuild company A's business.

3. Application of FRA

3.1 Procedure to build a profit and loss framework in FRA

In order to apply FRA, the first step is to set up customer segments by the degree of customer relationships, then allocate revenue and cost items by customer segments, and thereby build a profit and loss statement by customer segments.

3.2 *Classifying four customer segments*

Based on the customer lifecycle (see Figure 2), categorization of customers into four customer segments is organized as follows: (A) the new customers, (B) the repeat customers, (C) the variable customers, and (D) the defectors based on behaviors and purchase activities (see Tables 1 and 2).

3.3 *Profit and loss statement by customer segments*

3.3.1 *Procedure of building profit and loss statement by customer segments*

To build profit and loss statement, allocation of revenue and cost items according to customer segments are set in Section 3.2.

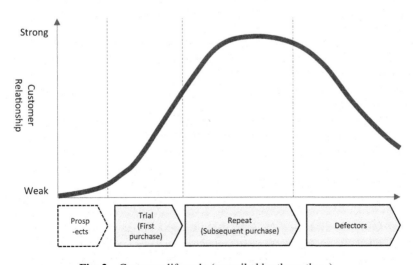

Fig. 2   Customer lifecycle (compiled by the authors).

Table 1. Customer segments criteria.

	Criteria 1			Criteria 2
(A) The New Customers	Elapsed days from the first purchase	Within 1 year		—
(B) The Repeat Customers		Over 1 year	Latest Purchase Activity	Within 1 year
(C) The Variable Customers				Between 1 and 2 years ago
(D) The Defectors				Over 2 years ago

Table 2. Number of customers and the ratio of company A.

	Number of Customers (Thousands)	Ratio in all segments (%)
(A) The New Customers	25	13.9%
(B) The Repeat Customers	25	13.9%
(C) The Variable Customers	28	15.6%
(D) The Defectors	102	56.7%

As for revenue, sales transaction data can be distinguished for each customer, and we can aggregate them for each customer segment.

Regarding costs, in Section 3.3.2, allocation of costs (other than the common cost) to each customer segment according to each cost item is given.

3.3.2 *Classify cost items*

In order to allocate cost items to each customer segment, we first classified sales cost, selling and administrative expenses, which is a major cost at company A, by the following three procedures:

(a)   Classify all costs into variable or fixed.
(b-1)   Classify variable cost into variable or semi-variable.

(b-2) Classify fixed costs into classifiable or unclassifiable such as common costs.

(c) Set cost-driver to allocate semi-variable and classifiable variable costs by customer segments.

Direct variable costs: Cost of goods (319 million JPY), including settlement fees such as credit cards and convenience store payments (14 million JPY), debt collection and bad debt expense (11 million JPY). About two-thirds (62.5%, 344 million JPY) of the total cost of 612 million JPY is a direct variable cost linked to sales, due to the characteristics of mail-order retailing business.

Semi-variable costs: Delivery costs, such as transportation and labor costs at a logistic base (49 million JPY), and order processing costs such as communication expenses by telephone, fax, postcard, and labor cost (22 million JPY). This share is about one-eighth of the total cost (12.9%, 71 million JPY), and set "number of orders" as cost-driver.

Classifiable fixed costs: Includes promotion expenses, mainly through distribution costs of catalogs for repeat customers (120 million JPY), acquiring expenses such as catalog distribution for new or prospective customers and internet advertisement costs (37 million JPY), warehouse rent, and IT systems expenses (10 million JPY). This accounts for about one-third of the total cost (30.3%, 167 million JPY).

Set cost-driver "number of customers" to promotion expenses, "number of acquisitions" to acquisition expense, "number of order" to warehouse and IT costs.

Unclassifiable fixed costs: Includes administration expenses such as administrative labor, office rent, and accounting systems costs (35 million JPY).

A summary of the classified cost items and annual amount is shown below (see Table 3).

3.3.3 *Build profit and loss statement*

Based on these conditions, we build the profit and loss statement (Table 4) by customer segments for the past year (*t* period: 2010/10–2011/9) before the M&A.

Table 3. Breakdown of all costs classified into three types, cost driver and annual amount.

Costs			Fixed/variable/ semi-variable	Classifiable/ unclassifiable	Cost driver	Annual Amount (million JPY)
Cost of sold	Costs of goods		Variable	—	—	319
	Costs of delivery		Semi-variable	—	Number of orders	49
Operation expense	promotion	Catalog	Fixed	Classifiable	Number of existing customers	120
		Acquiring	Variable	Classifiable	Number of newly acquired customers	37
	Order receiving process		Semi-variable	—	Number of orders	22
	Warehouse		Fixed	Classifiable	Number of orders	10
	Settlement		Variable	—	—	14
	Collection		Variable	—	—	11
	Administration		Fixed	Unclassifiable	—	35

Table 4. Income statement by customer segment.

(Million JPY)		Total	(1) New customers	(2) Repeat customers	(3) Variable customers	(4) Defectors
Number of Customers (thousands)		180	25	25	28	102
Revenues Ratio (%)		550	140	226	120	64
		100	25	41	22	12
1) Classifiable variable cost	Cost of goods sold	368	94	151	80	43
	Operation expenses	47	12	19	10	5
	Sub total	415	106	170	90	48
Marginal profit		135	34	55	29	16
2) Classifiable fixed cost	Cost of goods sold	—	—	—	—	—
	Operation expenses	167	56	38	40	32
	Sub total	167	56	38	40	32
Contribution margin		▲ 32	▲ 22	(a) 17	▲ 11	▲ 16
3) Unclassifiable fixed cost	Cost of goods sold	—				
	Operation expenses	35				
	Sub total	(b) 35				
Operation profit		▲ 67				
Fixed operation profit		▲ 18				

※ Fixed operation profit = (a) – (b)

4. Profitability Analysis

4.1 Marginal profit variance analysis

We allocate variable costs, totaling 415 million JPY, such as cost of goods, some commission fees, and operation costs into customer segments.

(1) New customers: 106 million JPY
(2) Repeat customers: 170 million JPY
(3) Variable customers: 90 million JPY
(4) Defectors: 48 million JPY

As a result, the marginal profit ratio to sales are calculated as follows:

(1) New customers: 24.5%
(2) Repeat customers: 24.7%
(3) Variable customers: 25.3%
(4) Defectors: 24.6%

There is no significant difference among customer segments; in other words, there is little difference due to differences in customer relationships.

4.2 Contribution margin difference analysis

We allocate classifiable fixed costs, totaling 167 million JPY, such as promotion costs, acquiring expense, warehouse rent, and IT system costs into customer segments.

(1) New customers: 56 million JPY
(2) Repeat customers: 38 million JPY
(3) Variable customers: 40 million JPY
(4) Defectors: 32 million JPY

As a result, the classifiable fixed cost ratio to sales are calculated as follows:

(1) New customers   39.9%
(2) Repeat customers: 16.5%
(3) Variable customers: 32.9%
(4) Defectors: 50.0%

Unlike variable costs, there were sufficient differences among customer segments (from 16.5% to 50.0%).
And contribution margin ratio to sales are as follows:

(1) New customers: −15.7%
(2) Repeat customers: 7.5%
(3) Variable customers: −9.2%
(4) Defectors: −25.0%

Due to the difference on the classifiable fixed cost ratio, there are adequate differences on contribution margins among customer segments.

Suzuki's (2007, p. 222) examination of a case in the retail industry led to the conclusion that "The contribution margin of fixed customers was about three points higher than variable customers".

In this study's case of company A as well, the profitability of repeat customers (fixed customers) is higher than other customer segments. However, the difference exceeded a maximum of 30 points, which was much higher than expected.

4.3 *Summary of profitability analysis findings*

The results of our profitability analysis yielded three findings.

First, we found that (2) repeat customers was the only customer segment with a positive profit contribution. Surprisingly, among the pre-acquisition customer segments, the profit contribution of even (3) variable customers, who were considered active customers, was negative.

In the case study of retailing (Suzuki, 2007), even though all customer segments were profitable (i.e., were making a positive profit contribution), the profitability of repeat customers was extremely high compared with that of other segments. "Although repeat customers comprised about 30% of total customers, they contributed about 80% of revenues and profits" (Suzuki, 2007). In the case of company A, although (2) repeat customers were profitable, the result was even more lopsided as this was the only profitable segment. The high proportion of corporate profitability from repeat customers was thus confirmed, in line with prior research (e.g., see Suzuki 2007).

Second, we did not observe large variations in variable costs by customer segment. The differences among segments came to less than 1% of

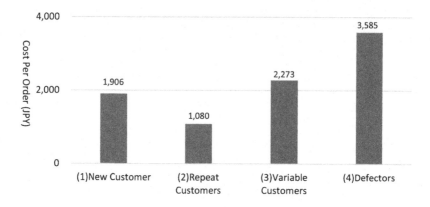

Fig. 3   CPO by customer segments.

sales. In the retailing case study by Suzuki (2007), excluding the break-even point for expenses, the percentage was 38.0% for non-repeat customers and 37.1% for repeat customers, or less than 1%. This is similar to our observations in the case of company A.

Third, it was clear that most of the differences between customer segments were attributable to the degree of linkage between sales and marketing promotion expenses for acquiring new customers and inducing repeat purchases.

Also, Figure 3 shows that cost per order (CPO), calculated by dividing marketing promotion expenses (157 million JPY) by the number of orders, is more than three times higher for (4) defectors than for (2) repeat customers.

Compared with typical retailers, such as supermarkets and department stores, the mail-order business is characterized by a high percentage of advertising and marketing promotion costs, which includes catalog costs.

5. Implications for Marketing Strategies

Based on the findings of the FRA profitability analysis discussed previously, efforts were made to improve company A's profitability by reducing various types of expenses, particularly the cost of goods and other variable costs. However, priority was placed on reviewing company A's marketing strategies, with a view to increasing the efficiency of marketing promotion expenses in particular, as such expenses comprised almost 30% of sales and accounted for almost all the differences in profitability by customer segment.

Furthermore, overall corporate profit greatly improved due to drastic cutbacks in marketing to target customers who were not likely to make repeat purchases, such as (4) defectors and (3) variable customers (i.e., unprofitable customer segments), in order to increase the efficiency of catalog production and distribution costs, which comprised about 90% of marketing promotion expenses.

In addition, the following three initiatives were adopted to further enhance the efficiency of marketing promotion expenses:

First was the acquisition of new customers with lower acquisition costs from among the paying customers from parent company B's existing businesses (job recruitment and advertising, publishing, operation of community websites, and other businesses targeting nurses and used by more than 300,000 nurses per year). However, due to concerns that personnel at company B would push back because efforts to assist company A would entail additional work for them and not be directly linked to their business performance, company B added assessment of intracompany transactions and strategy formulation and dissemination to its performance reviews.

Second was the reduction of catalog costs (production and distribution costs) by reviewing vendors and revamping the production process. Purchasing management had not taken any steps to compare cost estimates from several vendors, so the company's catalog costs were higher than prevailing market rates, leaving much room to cut costs.

As a result, the company succeeded in reducing its catalog unit cost of more than 300 JPY to less than two-thirds that amount.

Third was the improvement of online sales. The costs incurred from online sales basically include such systems-related costs as server operating expenses and system repair expenses, as well as content production, e-zine transmission, and other operating costs. Most of these are fixed costs, which show almost no increase with sales, order volumes, or the number of members. Therefore, cost efficiency improves as online sales increase.

Before the acquisition, company A's proportion of online sales was a paltry 5%. At that time, CPO was almost 2,000 JPY, so cost efficiency was poor. If additional investment could bring the ratio of online sales up to 30%, the CPO for online sales could go to 500 JPY, or 7.3% of sales, which would drastically reduce the ratio of marketing promotion expenses. The company therefore started pushing online sales to a much greater extent.

Within two years, as a result of these initiatives, the company was booking the majority (over 50%) of its sales online, which led to a vast improvement in post-acquisition financial performance.

6. The Limits of this Paper and Future Research Topics

This case study quantified whether differences exist in the profitability of various customer segments and the extent of such differences. Its findings have provided extremely valuable suggestions for determining the optimal allocation of expenses and other resources when rethinking marketing strategies in order to restore financial performance in a timely manner. Before its acquisition, company A had no data on profitability, so it was still sending catalogs to (4) defectors and (3) variable customers. The company thus decided to drastically reduce its catalog mailings.

However, in this case study of mail-order company A, most differences in profitability were due to marketing promotion expenses. The findings for other companies in the same industry or for other industries may differ, so of course the application of FRA profitability analysis would make different suggestions regarding marketing strategies and/or business strategies in those cases.

For future research projects, we would like to examine different case studies from other industry sectors to pursue a more coherent discussion of how FRA profitability analysis can be applied to business strategies.

References

Matsuoka, M. and Suzuki, K. 2008. A variance analysis in fixed revenue accounting: The framework and a case study for customer relationship variance analysis, *The Journal of Cost Accounting Research*, 32 (1), 85–97 (in Japanese).

Matsuoka, M. and Suzuki, K. 2009. Variance deployment based on the bathtub model framework in fixed revenue accounting, *The Journal of Cost Accounting Research*, 33 (2), 45–58 (in Japanese).

Ministry of Health, Labor and Welfare. 2014. Overview of medical facilities surveys and hospital reporting 2013, available at http://www.mhlw.go.jp/toukei/saikin/hw/iryosd/13/ (dated 2014.12.02) (in Japanese).

Suzuki, K. 2007. A consideration on the applicability of fixed revenue accounting, *The Accounting*, 171 (2), 46–57 (in Japanese).

Suzuki, K. 2012. Fixed revenue accounting, In (Eds.) Saki, A. and Suzuki, K. *A Study for Developing the New Models of Strategic Management Control*, Memoirs of the Institute of Social Sciences, Meiji University, Volume 50, issue 2, pp. 24–80 (in Japanese).

Chapter 3

Identifying the Determinant Factors Satisfying Each Customer Segment: Case of a Japanese Hotel Chain

Kayo Mitani and John Hatzinikolakis

1. Introduction

For a company to be able survive in a society where the competitive environment has intensified alongside internationalization, it is important that it builds good business relationships with its customers who provide it with revenue so they can be encouraged to repeatedly use its products or services. In other words, it is important to build and develop good relationships that satisfy both parties: transactions that satisfy customers, and that can also be expected to produce financial outcomes for the company (Mitani and Suzuki, 2015). In relationship marketing, which aims to build and develop relationships between companies and their customers (hereafter, "customer relationships"), it is necessary to segment customers according to the strength of the customer relationship, ascertain the factors that satisfy the customers in each of the customer segments (hereafter, determinant factors), and formulate and implement a strategy that satisfies these determinant factors (Anderson and Narus, 1991; Berry, 1995). This is based on the assumption that since the determinant factors for each customer segment are different, the financial outcomes obtained by satisfying each customer segment will also be different.

Therefore, a question may be asked as to whether the determinant factors really are different for each customer segment? Also, yet another question is whether customer satisfaction criteria of each customer segment have different effects on financial results? In particular, how do the determinant factors for regular customers, the customers with whom companies have strong customer relationships that they should maintain and acquire, and the effects on the financial results from their customer satisfaction, differ from those for customers in other segments? It is important to explore and answer these questions.

Therefore, in this study, in the customer segments with different customer relationships that are assumed for Company A in the hotel industry, the determinant factors and customer satisfaction, and their relationships with financial results, will be clarified. In addition, clarification will be sought on how the effects of customer satisfaction on financial results, and the determinant factors that produce the customer satisfaction, differ.

2. Prior Research

Interest in non-financial indicators of customer satisfaction has increased as a result of the Balanced Score Card (BSC) approach. Research studies verifying the causal relationship between customer satisfaction and financial results have been conducted in Japan and elsewhere (e.g., Ittner and Larcker, 1998; Banker *et al.* 2000; Matsuoka, 2006). Ittner and Larcker (1998) used data from a customer questionnaire survey conducted by a major U.S. telecommunications company, while Banker *et al.* (2000) used data on the hotel industry, and both showed that customer satisfaction is a leading indicator of financial results. Matsuoka (2006) used data on the hotel industry in Japan and showed that customer satisfaction affected the financial results of the relevant fiscal period.

Studies have also been conducted analyzing the determinant factors affecting customer satisfaction by showing the causal relationship between customer satisfaction and financial results. Behn and Riley (1999) used data from the U.S. aviation industry, while Smith and Wright (2004) used data on six major companies within the U.S. personal computer industry. Both studies showed that factors like service quality, brand strategy, and the competitiveness of the relevant company affected financial results, such as return on assets (ROA) and the sales growth rate, through customer satisfaction.

Behn and Riley (1999) and Smith and Wright (2004) used data at the corporate level and analyzed companies' customers after ascertaining the customers to be uniform. However, in recent years, analyses have also been conducted using data at the customer level on the basis that due to different customer relationships, the effects of determinant factors and customer satisfaction on financial results are different. Dikolli *et al.* (2007) suggested that by developing customer relationships, switching costs are increased for customers, which promotes repeat usage and thereby affects financial results. Matsuoka (2006) understood the strength of customer relationships to be the duration of the transaction period, and used it as one of the control variables for the analysis. However, from the results of this analysis, the transaction period was not found to have significant effect on the relationship between the determinant factors and customer satisfaction, or on the relationship between customer satisfaction and financial results.

Instead of the transaction period, Mitani and Suzuki (2015) analyzed the relationship among the determinant factors, customer satisfaction, and financial results by customer segment according to usage frequency on the basis that different services should be provided to each of the customer segments by the companies being surveyed. They set a model for customer satisfaction as the variable that mediates the determinant factors and financial results (customers' total monetary usage amount) based on the 4Ps of the marketing mix (product, price, place, and promotion), as proposed by McCarthy (1975), and carried out the verification. The results showed that the evaluation of ancillary facilities like hot springs among loyal customers with a strong customer relationship and the evaluation of all the facilities relating to the hotel room and atmosphere within the hotel among new customers with a weak relationship had major effects on customer satisfaction and that there was a statistically significant difference for the extent of the effects of these determinant factors on customer satisfaction. However, Mitani and Suzuki (2015) did not verify if there was a difference in the extent of the effects of customer satisfaction on financial results in each customer segment. Moreover, to measure the financial results, they used the total annual usage monetary amount by customer and did not consider that there are different cost structures in each of the hotels frequented by the customers or the characteristics of customers who have strong customer relationships with the companies under study.

Issues also remained with the setting of the determinant factors. The debate on the marketing mix is being advanced, and it is recognized that in the service industry, which includes intangible services, the marketing mix is not limited to the 4Ps but comprises the 7Ps(the addition of people, process, and physical evidence). The importance of intangible services has been actively discussed in the marketing field, and in Garbarino and Johnson (1999), from the questionnaire data of customers of a New York theater company, it was suggested that among customers with strong relationships, services that relate to the psychological aspect of the customer–employee interaction is important. Zhang *et al.* (2016) also stressed that in order to move customers into a customer segment with a strong customer relationship, it is necessary to strengthen services relating to this psychological aspect. However, in the debate within marketing, there has been insufficient investigation of its relationship with financial results, so doubts remain on whether strengthening this factor will have the effect of improving companies' financial results.

3. Research Design

3.1 *Analytical model*

In this study, whether the determinant factors for each customer segment with different customer relationships, and the effects on financial results of the customer satisfaction resulting from them, are different, shall be clarified. Based on Mitani and Suzuki's research (2015), who analyzed the determinant factors in each customer segment with different customer relationships, customer satisfaction, and financial results, a model of customer satisfaction as a variable that mediates determinant factors and financial results was established.

This study targets the hotel industry as the research site, so it was considered appropriate to adopt the 7Ps, as it is the marketing mix of the service industry. Also, in addition to transaction data by customer from Company A, data on profitability by the hotel group was acquired. Thus, for financial results, the amount of profit by customer was used instead of the total customer annual usage amount.

3.2 Research site

Company A, which operates a chain of hotels within Japan, was chosen as the research site. Company A has dozens of hotels within Japan, and it develops luxury hotels targeting wealthy customers. It regularly conducts both employee satisfaction surveys and customer satisfaction questionnaire surveys, and it is a company that is highly interested in non-financial indicators.

There were two reasons for selecting Company A. First, in addition to the questionnaire left in the hotel guest rooms, it conducts an annual customer questionnaire survey for those customers who have registered as members, which meant it was easy to acquire customer questionnaire survey data. Moreover, as it has adopted a membership system, it was also possible to obtain transaction data by customer. The second reason was that Company A feels the need to analyze customer questionnaire survey data by customer segment. Up to the present time, Company A has focused its efforts into acquiring new customers through constructing new hotels. The results of the customer questionnaire survey each year would only confirm changes to the numbers on the point that the customer satisfaction of existing customers was not being damaged, so the survey had been reduced to being in form only. However, within Japan, Company A had come to realize the limits to acquiring new customers from within the customer segment that it was targeting. It has thus turned its attention toward existing customers, which it had not focused on that much, and in the last few years it has become increasingly aware of aiming to develop customer relationships. In order to effectively develop customer relationships, it is necessary to divide customer segments through the strength of customer relationships. This is so that a company is able to ascertain each segment's determinant factors and the effects of its customer satisfaction on financial results, formulate a strategy that can be expected to improve financial results, and make decisions on the efficient allocation of resources. From this background, Company A needed to analyze the differences in the relationship among each customer segment's determinant factors, customer satisfaction, and financial results, and therefore it can be said that it was appropriate as the research site for this study's aims and questions.

3.3 *Setting the customer segments*

Questions on how to measure the strength of customer relationships and set the customer segments are the essential ones to be discussed while considering the conditions of the relevant company. The Management Planning Department of Company A, responsible for analyzing the customer questionnaire survey, has used variables in which customers are divided into ranks based on usage frequency. It sets customers with an annual usage frequency of 13 times or more as the highest ranked customer segment. This customer segment is made up of customers who are expected to produce financial results for Company A. These customers want to be guests in the hotels frequently. Thus, it can be inferred that they are patrons with a strong relationship with Company A, as a relationship of satisfaction has been established for both the company and for the customers. Although this classification method utilizing usage frequency was not recognized throughout the entire company, customers who use the hotel once, twice, or more in a month were recognized as being important customers for the hotels owned by Company A. In this study, it was thus decided to use customer classification variables and the number of transactions held by Company A's Management Planning Department to determine the customer segments based on different customer relationship strengths. The customer segments based on strength of customer relationship were comprised of a strong relationship customer segment with an annual usage frequency of 13 or more nights, and a weak relationship segment with an annual usage frequency of less than 13 nights.

3.4 *The data and the analytical method*

The subjects of the analysis were the 1,789 people who answered the fiscal year (FY) 2015 customer questionnaire survey. For the FY 2015 customer questionnaire survey, approximately 5,800 questionnaires were sent to randomly selected customers. Among the 1,789 people who answered the questionnaire, data from those who did not use Company A's hotels in FY 2015 was excluded, leaving 1,652 respondents as the subject of the analysis. Furthermore, based on Company A's classification method, the customers were then divided into regular customers with a strong customer relationship with an annual usage frequency of 13 times or more; non-regular customers with a weak customer relationship with an annual usage frequency of less than 13 times; and, new customers who became members during FY 2015. As a result, there were 127 regular customers, 723 non-regular customers, and 802 new customers. In all customer segments, the largest age group were those in their 60s (regular customers: approximately 34.4%, non-regular customers: 34.6%, new customers: 32.7%), followed by those in their 50s (regular customers: approximately 25.4%, non-regular customers: 23%, new customers: 23.4%). By gender, in all of the customer segments, males were the majority and constituted approximately 60% of all respondents.

In the analysis of this study, the fiscal 2015 transaction data by customer and data from the customer questionnaire survey for FY 2015 were used. The aforementioned customer questionnaire survey adopted a 5-level Likert scale. In addition, data on profitability by hotel was also obtained from Company A. To measure financial results, the total annual usage monetary amounts by customer were used. Using customer transaction data, the hotels at which these usage monetary amounts were used were identified, and the calculations were carried out by multiplying them by the relevant profit ratio.

The 7Ps of the services marketing mix were used as determinant factors and were measured as follows:

For Product, the factors were set as the evaluation of all the facilities measured from three question items on the atmosphere and usability of the facility and the hotel guest rooms, and the evaluation of ancillary facilities measured from three question items asking the respondent to evaluate the hot spring facilities attached to the hotel. Since these variables also include concepts to evaluate Physical evidence (e.g., interior decor and spaces), it was decided to use these two variables to analyze and measure both the concepts of Product and Physical evidence.

For Price, the factors consisted of two question items in which the respondents were asked to evaluate the accommodation packages that Company A offers to customers. Because the packaged services offered by Company A enable the facilities to be used more inexpensively than the usual price, they were considered suitable to measure the evaluation of Company A's pricing strategy.

For Promotion, the factors consisted of four question items asking for an evaluation of the promotional activities conducted by Company A.

For People, the factors were set from two viewpoints — staff abilities and staff friendliness. There were five question items asking for an evaluation of the hotel employee abilities in terms of the correctness/precision of the services rendered by the hotel staff. For friendliness, there were three question items related to whether the guests felt that the hotel employees were friendly and whether they responded to them in an attentive manner.

For Process, the factor was set as the evaluation of the "responsible person" — the one who was responsible in guiding the hotel and accommodation packages to a customer and who makes the reservation. This consisted of three question items asking for an evaluation of the person responsible for the provision of information on hotel facilities and promoting their use to customers registered as members. As there were no question items that could measure Place (channel), it was decided not to use it in the analysis in this study.

Customer satisfaction consisted of a total of six question items: two question items asking for an evaluation solely from the actual use of Company A's hotels; a question item asking on the intention to use them again, and three question items asking on the intention to recommend the hotels to other people. These variables were measured by a confirmatory factor analysis using Amos. In the results of the confirmatory factor analysis, $\chi^2 = 5619.554$, df $= 1110$, $p = 0.000$, CFI $= 0.848$, and RMSEA $= 0.050$, and excellent goodness of data fit were obtained. Tables 1 and 2 show the variables' correlations and the descriptive statistics. In order to comply with confidentiality obligations, the profit amounts were treated in such a way so that the characteristics of the data were not adversely affected.

As with Mitani and Suzuki (2015), the customer segments were recognized to be separate populations, and so a multi-population analysis was adopted during the analysis of the relationships among the measured determinant factors, customer satisfaction, and financial results. The analysis was then progressed in accordance with the following two steps:

First, the invariance of the factors was confirmed. Factor invariance pertains to the extent to which the same factor can be measured between

Table 1. The variables' correlations.

	All facilities	Ancillary facilities	Staff abilities	Staff friendliness	Responsible person	Advertising	Accommodation packages	Customer satisfaction
All facilities	1							
Ancillary facilities	0.395**	1						
Staff abilities	0.719**	0.352**	1					
Staff friendliness	0.553**	0.309**	0.660**	1				
Responsible person	0.307**	0.242**	0.346**	0.531**	1			
Advertising	0.250**	0.210**	0.258**	0.262**	0.252**	1		
Accommodation packages	0.250**	0.204**	0.285**	0.286**	0.239**	0.173**	1	
Customer satisfaction	0.522**	0.361**	0.527**	0.562**	0.423**	0.297**	0.352**	1
Profit amount	0.133**	0.066**	0.086**	0.115**	0.187**	0.060**	0.128**	0.195**

Notes: ***$p < 0.001$, **$p < 0.01$, *$p < 0.05$, +$p < 0.10$

Table 2. The variables' descriptive statistics in each customer segment.

	New customer (N = 802)		Non-regular customers (N = 723)		Regular customers (N = 127)	
	Mean	Standard deviation	Mean	Standard deviation	Mean	Standard deviation
All facilities	4.12	0.69	4.11	0.67	4.22	0.62
Ancillary facilities	4.37	0.70	4.38	0.66	4.36	0.68
Staff abilities	4.12	0.71	4.13	0.72	4.14	0.71
Staff friendliness	3.92	0.86	3.97	0.89	4.05	0.93
Responsible person	3.69	1.10	3.70	1.11	3.97	1.11
Advertising	2.97	0.81	2.99	0.84	3.06	0.85
Accommodation packages	3.07	0.95	3.10	0.95	3.46	1.04
Customer satisfaction	3.63	0.78	3.69	0.74	3.93	0.69
Profit amount	6,173.52	6,687.11	4,996.01	4,411.92	16,465.25	9,638.79

populations. Here, the goodness of fit of the data with a model (measurement invariant model) with a condition and with a model without any type of condition (placement invariant model) were verified and compared. The model with a condition has an equality condition, where the load amounts of each factor are equal between the customer segments (the path coefficient extending from the factor to the question item, as the observation variable) (Kano and Miura, 2002).

Second, the results of the model with the best fit with the data was adopted, and the differences in the customer segments were verified from testing the values of the path coefficients to customer satisfaction of the estimated determinant factors and of the path coefficients to the financial results from customer satisfaction, and their differences.

4. Results of the Analysis and Considerations

In the results of multi-population analysis using the placement invariant model and the measurement invariant model, $\chi^2 = 5651.528$, df = 1131, $p = 0.00$, CFI = 0.848, and RMSEA = 0.049 in the placement invariant model, while in the measurement invariant model, $\chi^2 = 5730.607$, df = 1173, $p = 0.00$, CFI = 0.847, and RMSEA = 0.049. Both models showed excellent goodness of fit for CFI and RMSEA. However, the value of AIC showing the relative goodness of fit for the models' analysis data was lower for the measurement invariant model (placement invariant model = 6359.528, measurement invariant model = 6354.607, respectively), and the fit with the data was good. The results of the test of the path coefficients between the variables in each customer segment estimated from the measurement invariant model, and also their differences, are as shown in Table 3.

The results of the analysis confirmed that in the relationship between customer satisfaction and financial results, customer satisfaction has a statistically significant positive effect on regular customers (0.159), non-regular customers (0.221), and new customers (0.166), respectively. However, in each of the customer segments, no significant difference was observed in the size of the impact of customer satisfaction on the financial results (path coefficient). Differences were not found in the effects of customer satisfaction on financial results among customer segments.

Table 3. Results of the test of the path coefficients and the differences by customer segment.

		New customers		Non-regular customers		Regular customers	
		Standardizing coefficient	Standard deviation	Standardizing coefficient	Standard deviation	Standardizing coefficient	Standard deviation
Customer satisfaction	← All facilities	0.237***z	0.068	0.435***z	0.079	0.326*	0.155
	← Ancillary facilities	0.122**	0.033	0.07+	0.030	0.201*	0.076
	← Staff abilities	−0.022	0.048	−0.113	0.059	0.171	0.122
	← Staff friendliness	0.409***z	0.042	0.301***z	0.039	−0.062	0.095
	← Responsible person	0.049	0.021	0.126***z	0.019	0.327**z	0.580
	← Advertising	0.09*	0.034	0.082*	0.031	0.044	0.07
	← Accommodation packages	0.112***	0.022	0.138***	0.022	0.910	0.041
Profit Amount	← Customer satisfaction	0.166***	338.393	0.221***	295.720	0.159+	1533.556

Notes: ***p < 0.001, **p < 0.01, *p < 0.05, + p < 0.10.
z indicates that a significant difference was observed.

Furthermore, it was not found that customer satisfaction from a customer segment with a strong customer relationship affects financial results more than customer satisfaction of other segments.

Between customer satisfaction and determinant factors, it was gleaned that there are significant differences in the values of the path coefficients among the customer segments on evaluating the facilities overall, staff friendliness, and the responsible person (for making the booking, etc.). For facilities in general, a significant difference was observed between non-regular customers (0.435) and new customers (0.237), and it can be seen that non-regular customers place greater importance on the extent of the fulfillment of satisfaction by ancillary facilities versus new customers. This is a different result from that obtained by Mitani and Suzuki (2015). This is considered to be related to the fact that Company A has been opening new hotels. In the last few years, Company A has opened new hotels with different formats every year. It is considered that this opening of new hotels not only contributes to the acquisition of new customers but also to improvement of customer satisfaction of existing customers, particularly non-regular customers with weaker customer relationships. This is because it improves their customer satisfaction by providing them with new choices in terms of facilities as compared to previous choices up to that time.

For staff friendliness, a significant difference was seen between non-regular customers (0.301) and new customers (0.409), and it was discovered that new customers are easier to satisfy though staff friendliness, compared to non-regular customers. This is a different result from marketing research that argues that staff friendliness is a factor mostly important to customers with strong customer relationships. The height of the awareness in Company A about responding attentively to customers can be cited as the reason for this. Company A has adopted a membership system, wherein all of its hotels the names of the customers staying in its respective hotels are confirmed at a meeting every morning, and guidance is given in terms of managing the customers' information, their requirements and complaints during past use of Company A's hotels. It can be seen that despite using a specific hotel for the first time as a new customer, these customers are surprised by and feel satisfaction from the staff calling them by their name and being aware in advance of information such as their birthdays. Conversely, for non-regular customers, it is thought that during their repeated usage, they come to take the provision of such services for granted, and therefore the effects of service provisions on their customer satisfaction are lower in impact than for new customers.

In the evaluation of the responsible person, a significant difference was observed between regular customers (0.327) and new customers (0.126), and it was seen that regular customers place greater importance on interactions with the responsible person than new customers. It is thought that this is related to the fact that as the frequency of using the hotel increases, there is a corresponding increase in the number of interactions with the responsible person, such as for reservations, guidance, and inquiries.

5. Conclusion

In this study, the differences in the relationships between the determinant factors in each customer segment that have different strengths of customer relationships and customer satisfaction, and between customer satisfaction and financial results, were analyzed, interpreted, and clarified. In the results of this analysis, in all of the segments, it was found that as customer satisfaction rises, the profit amount increases. However, no statistical difference was observed in the extent of this effect among the customer segments. In the study's analysis, the customer segments were set using hotel usage frequency, which is the classification method used by Company A.

It can be suggested that the results of the analysis suggests the importance of searching for new methods for segmenting customers. It was found that there are differences in the determinant factors among the customer segments, and therefore the focus of one customer segment's marketing mix should be different from others'.

The significance of this study can be summarized in two points. The first point is in the implementation of relationship marketing. This study further reinforces the argument that a company should set its customer segments based on the strength of the relationship between a company and its customers (customer relationships), and focus its marketing strategy on meeting the differing needs of each customer segment. The second point is that the management control of companies that adopt relationship marketing should be conducted according to the different marketing strategies for each customer segment. Importantly, this study also clarifies that when evaluating the extent of the achievement of this strategy, it is necessary to measure and evaluate it for each customer segment.

In this study, the relationship between customer satisfaction and the profit amount, which had not been verified in previous research, was clarified using data at the customer level, and it can be said that it has advanced research on customer satisfaction within the field of management accounting research.

Finally, the limitations of this study and the issues to be addressed in future research are addressed in the following three points. One consideration is that this study is a case study of Company A in the hotel industry in Japan. It will be necessary to conduct analyses of other companies and other industries as well in order to compare and contrast results. Another factor to consider is the suitability of the method for segmenting the customers. In this study's analysis, the method of classification already being used by Company A was adopted, but further investigation is needed in order to consider its relation to a variety of factors in terms of how to convert customers to those with strong relationships with the company. A third consideration is that due to the data constraints in the analysis, a time lag between the determinant factors and customer satisfaction and the financial results was not assumed. This is an issue that is endeavored to be addressed and overcome in future research.

References

Anderson, J. C. and Narus J. A. 1991. Partnering as a Focused Market Strategy, *California Management Review*, 33, 95–113.

Banker, R. D., Potter, G., and Srinivasan, D. 2000. An Empirical Investigation of an Incentive Plan that Includes Nonfinancial Performance Measures, *The Accounting Review*, 75(1), 65–92.

Behn, B. K. and Riley, R. A. 1999. Using Nonfinancial Information to Predict Financial Performance: The Case of the US Airline Industry, *Journal of Accounting, Auditing & Finance*, 14(1), 29–56.

Berry, L. L. 1995. Relationship Marketing of Services—Growing Interest, Emerging Perspectives, *Journal of the Academy of Marketing Science*, 23(4), 236–245.

Dikolli, S. S., Kinney, W. R., and Sedatole, K. L. 2007. Measuring customer relationship value: the role of switching cost. *Contemporary Accounting Research*, 24(1), 93–132.

Garbarino, E., and Johnson, M. S. 1999. The Different Roles of Satisfaction, Trust, and Commitment in Customer Relationships, *Journal of Marketing*, 63(2), 70–87.

Ittner, C. D. and Larcker, D. F. 1998. Are Nonfinancial Measures Leading Indicators of Financial Performance? An Analysis of Customer Satisfaction, *Journal of Accounting Research*, 36, 1–35.

Kano, Y. and M. Miura. 2002. *Graphical Multivariate Analysis by AMOS, EQS, and CALIS: A Visual Covariance Structure Analysis*, Kyoto: Gendai-Sugakusha (In Japanese).

Matsuoka, K. 2006. Empirical research on the relationship between non-financial indicators and financial results, *Osaka Economic Papers*, 55(4), 106–126 (In Japanese).

McCarthy, E. J., Shapiro, S. J., and W. D. Perreault. 1975. Basic marketing. Georgetown, Ont.: Irwin-Dorsey."

Mitani, K. and Suzuki, K. 2015. Differences in the Determinant Factors of Customer Satisfaction in Customer Segments with Different Strengths of Customer Relationships, *The International Academy of Strategic Management*, 3(5), 401–418 (In Japanese).

Smith, R. E. and Wright, W. F. 2004. Determinants of Customer Loyalty and Financial Performance, *Journal of Management Accounting Research*, 16(1), 183–205.

Zhang, J. Z., Watson IV, G. F., Palmatier, R. W., and Dant, R. P. 2016. Dynamic Relationship Marketing, *Journal of Marketing*, 80(5), 53–57.

Part 2
Stability Analysis

Chapter 4

Measuring and Managing Customer Profit Stability: A Japanese Hotel Chain Case Study

Ayuko Komura and Kenichi Suzuki

1. Introduction

It is important for companies to be able to secure stable profit. It is, for example, easier for a company to procure funds if investors and banks judge the company to be stable with steadily increasing net profit each term (Trueman and Titman, 1988; Martinez and Castro, 2011; Li and Richie, 2016). Additionally, by lowering the cost of capital, stable profits increase shareholder value (Srivastava *et al.*, 1997; Suzuki *et al.*, 2006). Stable operating profits also allow for continuous investment and employment (Bloom *et al.*, 2007). Furthermore, it improves the accuracy of forecasts of next term's earnings based on current-term earnings (Niimi, 2011; Komura and Suzuki, 2014). Indeed, according to research by Graham *et al.* (2005), in which the authors surveyed Chief Financial Officers of 312 listed US companies and interviewed an additional 20 Chief Financial Officers, 96.9% of respondents preferred stable profits to fluctuating profits.

We focus on the stability of operating profits within overall profit stability because it seems that ensuring stable operating profits from core businesses stabilizes net profit. Additionally, Niimi (2011) indicates that when considering profit stability, it is best to exclude one-off profit items such as extraordinary losses and gains.

What should firms do to ensure that they secure a stable operating profit? Past management accounting studies discuss the impact of cost composition (the ratio of fixed to variable costs) on operating profit stability. Indeed, Lev (1974; 1983) verifies it. In other words, prior studies show that the higher the ratio of fixed costs within a company's overall costs, the more variable its operating profit is.

Studies of fixed revenue accounting (FRA)[1] explain that, in addition to cost composition, the relative weight of the contributory margin from the fixed customer segment and that from customers besides fixed customers (the non-fixed customer segment) influences operating profit stability. Fixed customers are those who are not overly susceptible to competitors' actions (such as new product launches, advertising, or other sales promotion activity) and are likely to continue to do business with the company in the future because they are satisfied with the company's products or services and are loyal to the company (Srivastava et al., 1998). Consequently, profits from fixed customers are more stable than profits from non-fixed customers (Suzuki, 2005).

Thus, it is conceivable that if a company can acquire stable profits from fixed customers, the more it increases its profits from these customers; that is, the more it increases the contributory margin attributable to the fixed customer segment within the overall contributory margin, the more stable its operating profit will be. However, that there has been insufficient investigation into whether profits from fixed customers are inherently stable based on actual cases is an issue.

Thus, our intention is to use a case study of a Japanese hotel chain as a research site to verify whether the company experiences higher stable profits from fixed customers with high transaction sustainability within a certain period than that from non-fixed customers. Operating profit stability due to the creation and maintenance of fixed customers is also examined.

This paper proceeds as follows. First, Section 2 establishes the analysis model from prior research. Section 3 outlines the research design.

---

[1] FRA is accounting for management control, with dynamic implementation of relationship marketing strategies, by measuring the impact of transaction relationships with customers on financial outcomes (Suzuki, 2005).

Section 4 reports and discusses the analysis. Finally, in Section 5, a summary of the report, its limitations, and issues for future research are shown.

2. Hypothesis

2.1 *Marginal profit stability by customer type*

In FRA, customers are classified as new, fixed, non-fixed, and defectors depending on their relationship with the company. This method aggregates sales, variable costs, and fixed costs per customer segment and calculates the contributory margin of each customer segment. However, in this study, because our discussion addresses the profit attributable to each individual customer rather than to each customer segment, marginal profit per customer is focused. This is because when profits are calculated per customer, it is difficult to allocate customer segment fixed costs to individual customers.

In addition, we chose to measure the stability of a customer's marginal profit using the correlation between the marginal profit by customer for the term in question and the following term. This is because it is reasonable to expect that, if the marginal profit is stable, then, when we measure the next term's marginal profit against the current term's marginal profit, there will be no great difference between the two, and thus there will be a high correlation between them.

2.2 *Relationship between profit stability with fixed customer classification in fixed revenue accounting*

In FRA, fixed customers are defined as "customers with high transaction sustainability within a certain period" (Suzuki, 2005, p. 164). Suzuki (2005) outlines the following two relevant classification methods.

The first method identifies fixed customers by measuring transaction sustainability based on customers' individual transaction data within a certain period. For example, customers with many transactions within a period are classified as fixed customers. The second method identifies customers' inclination to sustain transactions using a questionnaire and classifies customers as fixed customers based on the results of the questionnaire.

Previous research tests whether profits from fixed customers defined using the questionnaire method are stable. For example, some studies report high stability of sales and gross profits attributable to satisfied and/ or loyal customers (Tarasi *et al.*, 2013; Komura, 2014) and that the more customers a company or a business has with a high degree of satisfaction and loyalty, the more stable its profits (Gruca and Rego, 2005; Suzuki *et al.*, 2006). Thus, it is not unreasonable to expect to generate stable profits from fixed customers by creating good relationships with them, having identified them as customers who are satisfied and have a high inclination to sustain transactions via a relevant questionnaire.

However, some companies may find it hard to use a survey to identify such customers. In that case, firms can classify customers as fixed based on their individual transaction data, as in the first method. Companies that introduced and implemented FRA classify customers as fixed according to the number of transactions (retailers, hotels) or number of years over which transactions are sustained (electronic component manufacturer) (Suzuki, 2007). That said, these studies do not verify the stability of the contribution margin from fixed customers using individual customer transaction data.

Hypothesis: The correlation of the marginal profit in the term in question attributable to the Fixed Customer Segment (classified using customers' individual transaction data) with the equivalent marginal profit in the following term being higher than the correlation of marginal profit in the term in question attributable to the Non-fixed Customer Segment with equivalent marginal profit in the following term.

3. Research Design

3.1 *Research site*

A Japanese hotel chain operator, Company A, is selected as our research site. Company A operates luxury hotels that are leisure destinations, with guests enjoying meals in the many restaurants (Japanese, Italian, French, Chinese, etc.), bathing in the hot springs, and receiving beauty treatments and massages.

Our reasons for selecting Company A as our research site were two-fold. First, stability of operating profit is an important issue for hotels.

Operating hotels is a fixed cost-style business, and the company can easily incur heavy losses if sales are not above the breakeven point (Dittman *et al.*, 2009). Thus, it is important to obtain a steady marginal profit at a level that can securely cover fixed costs. The employees in Company A's hotels consider customers who stay many times each year to be fixed customers and behave accordingly; for example, actively providing friendly service during their stay, such as calling them by their name.

Our second reason for selecting Company A is that it collects transaction data by customer and classifies customers as fixed customers according to the number of nights stayed in a year. Customers need to register as Company A members before staying at Company A's hotels, and membership numbers allow the company to integrate, monitor, and attribute data for each customer, such as age, address, and date of registration, with the transaction value at each hotel for each period.

3.2 *Data and sample selection*

In our analysis, we utilize:

(1) transaction data by customer between January 1, 2014 and December 31, 2015 (for each customer, number of nights stayed, name of hotel, and transaction value),
(2) attribute data at the time of registration as a member (such as the customer's date of birth, address, membership rank, and household income), and
(3) data from the general ledger of each hotel for 2014 and 2015.

Please note that in 2014 and 2015, the company operated 15 hotels, all of them in Japan.

As our sample, we first selected customers already registered as members at Company A's hotels on or before January 1, 2014, and who did not begin the process of withdrawing from membership from January 1, 2014 to December 31, 2015. Next, customers who stayed at Company A's hotels for at least one night between January 1 and December 31, 2014 and one night between January 1 and December 31, 2015 are selected. After this sample selection process, a total sample of 51,075 customers is used in our analysis.

3.3 Analysis method

3.3.1 Classification of customer segments at Company A

We classified the full sample into five segments using Company A's fixed customer and non-fixed customer segment categories, and carried out the regression analysis below. This operation allowed us to confirm the impact of classification as fixed customer and non-fixed customer on the stability of a customer's marginal profit based on transaction data.

The five segments were based on the number of nights stayed in 2014. Segment 1 includes customers who stayed at least 13 nights in 2014, Segment 2 includes customers who stayed 9–12 nights, Segment 3 includes customers who stayed 6–8 nights, Segment 4 includes customers who stayed 3–5 nights, and Segment 5 includes customers who stayed 1–2 nights. Company A considers customers in Segment 1 as fixed customers, with the highest transaction sustainability.[2]

Table 1 reports the basic statistics for each segment. To observe our duty of confidentiality to Company A, we report the average and standard deviation values of marginal profit in 2014 and 2015 for each segment as an index with the value for Segment 1 taken to be 100. The next section explains number of years of membership and membership rank.

3.3.2 Analysis model and variables

For each segment, we carried out a regression analysis using the following multiple regression equation.[3]

---

[2]Customer segments in FRA are based on the four categories of new customers, fixed customers, non-fixed customers, and defectors. However, since our analysis covered customers registered as members in or before 2014, we excluded New Customers from our analysis. Additionally, we excluded customers undertaking membership withdrawal procedure in 2014 or 2015, and customers not staying even one night in Company A's hotels in 2014 and 2015. We also excluded defectors from the analysis. In other words, the analysis in this study verifies the difference in the stability of the marginal profit attributable to fixed and non-fixed customers.

[3]We made selections regarding control variables within the explanatory variables in the multiple regression equation after carrying out multiple regression analysis using the stepwise method for the whole sample. The following variables were control variable candidates, but were excluded: (1) customer's age in 2014 and (2) customer's area of residence.

Table 1. Basic statistics by segment.

	Number of customers	No. of nights stayed (2014)	Marginal profit (2015)		Marginal profit (2014)		No. of yrs of membership		Membership rank	
			Mean	Standard deviation	Mean	Standard deviation	Mean	Standard deviation	Mean	Standard deviation
Segment One	10,409	13 or more	100.00	100.00	100.00	100.00	9.93	6.59	2.42	1.06
Segment Two	7,593	9–12 nights	50.26	38.86	42.64	20.62	9.30	6.29	2.24	1.02
Segment Three	9,372	6–8 nights	38.08	29.99	28.50	16.93	9.20	6.38	2.17	1.01
Segment Four	13,934	3–5 nights	27.42	21.89	16.25	8.79	9.32	6.54	2.09	0.99
Segment Five	9,767	1–2 nights	20.25	23.11	6.73	4.07	9.39	6.80	2.00	0.97

$$P_{i,2015} = \beta_0 + \beta_1 P_{i,2014} + \beta_2 X_{1,i,2014} + \beta_3 X_{2,i} + \varepsilon_i \qquad (1)$$

$P_{i,2015}$: Marginal profit of Customer i in 2015.
$P_{i,2014}$: Marginal profit of Customer i in 2014.
$X_{1,i,2014}$: Number of years of membership of Customer i in 2014 (control variable).
$X_{2,i}$: Membership rank of Customer i (control variable).

We test the hypothesis by whether the regression coefficient resulting from the regression analysis of the 2014 marginal profit of customers in Segment 1 is higher than the equivalent regression coefficient for customers in Segments 2–5.

Here, we calculate marginal profit by customer in the following way from Company A's transaction data by customer and data from the general ledger at each hotel. First, we use the individual accounting item method to separate the hotel's cost of goods sold and SG&A expenses (extracted from each hotel's general ledger for 2014 and 2015) into fixed and variable costs,[4] and calculated the marginal profit rate for each hotel (15 hotels) in 2014 and 2015. Next, we apply the annual marginal profit rate of the hotel in which each customer stayed to the sum they spent during their stay (transaction value by customer) to calculate the marginal profit attributable to that customer for each hotel stay. Finally, for each customer, we sum the marginal profit for each stay to arrive at a figure for total marginal profit per customer for 2014 and for 2015.[5]

Please note that we also asked about customers' income at the time of membership registration. However, few customers originally recorded their income at the time of registration, and these values were not updated, despite the possibility that income at registration in 2015 may differ significantly from income at registration in 2014. Thus, we did not investigate income as a possible control variable.

[4]There was a prior investigation at Company A into whether to treat the accounting items under SG&A expenses at hotels as variable or fixed costs, and we separated them into fixed and variable costs using a table provided.

[5]The rate of profit for each customer could differ in that there is a difference between customers using Company A's hotels after direct marketing by mail or telephone by Company A and customers using Company A's hotels with no prior guidance, and in that some customers require careful service during a stay and others who do not, and customers who often order high-margin wine and customers who do not. However, given the

We incorporated the number of years of a customer's membership in 2014 into the analysis as a control variable.

According to a member of the corporate planning team at Company A, in the first few years after becoming a member, customers use Company A's hotels frequently, but there is a tendency for the number of customers who cease to use Company A's hotels to increase as the number of years of membership grows. We can assume that this has an impact on the correlation of the marginal profit in 2014 and in 2015, and we therefore include it in the analysis to control for that impact.

We incorporate Customer i's membership rank into the analysis as a control variable. Membership rank refers to the four types of memberships Company A offers and have numerical labels of 1–4. Customers in membership rank four pay the highest annual membership fees and have the privilege of being able to use all of Company A's hotels at members' rates. As the numerical value of the rank label declines, the annual membership fees fall, and the customer can use fewer hotels at member rates. In other words, it is possible that because the higher the numerical label of a customer's membership rank, the more of Company A's various hotels they can use, membership rank would influence the correlation between relevant marginal profit in 2014 and in 2015.

4. Results and Discussion

Table 2 reports the analysis results.

The regression coefficient ($P_{i,2014}$) of the 2014 marginal profit by customer for Segment 1 (customers who spent at least 13 nights at Company A's hotels in 2014; Company A classifies these as fixed customers) was 0.727. This is higher than the regression coefficient of marginal profit by customer for Segment 2 (0.201), Segment 3 (0.136), Segment 4 (0.201), and Segment 5 (0.101). In other words, the annual marginal profit attributable to fixed customers who spend at least 13 nights at Company A's hotels is more stable that the marginal profit attributable to non-fixed Customers. Therefore, we believe that the hypothesis "The correlation of

---

restrictions of the data used, we arrived at a marginal profit rate per customer by applying the marginal profit rate for the hotels at which they stated to their transaction value.

Table 2.   Results of multiple regression analysis of each segment.

No. of nights stayed (2014)	Segment One 13 nights or more	Segment Two 9–12 nights	Segment Three 6–8 nights	Segment Four 3–5 nights	Segment Five 1–2 nights
Marginal profit (2014)	0.727*** (105.70)	0.201*** (17.03)	0.136*** (13.10)	0.202*** (23.85)	0.101*** (9.92)
No. of yrs. of membership (2014)	0.008 (1.23)	−0.063*** (−5.73)	−0.081*** (−8.04)	−0.089*** (−10.94)	−0.139*** (−13.98)
Membership rank	0.012⁺ (1.73)	0.147*** (12.48)	0.178*** (17.10)	0.142*** (16.79)	0.128*** (12.57)
Adj. R2	0.53	0.09	0.08	0.09	0.06
n	10,409	7,593	9,372	13,934	9,767

Notes: *** $p < 0.001$, ⁺ $p < 0.1$
Figures in parentheses are t values

the marginal profit in the term in question attributable to the Fixed Customer Segment (classified using customers' individual transaction data) with the equivalent marginal profit in the following term is higher than the correlation of marginal profit in the term in question attributable to the Non-fixed Customer Segment with equivalent marginal profit in the following term" is supported at Company A.

Company A always recognized the high profitability of fixed customers, and the fact that the results show that the relevant marginal profit remains stable and enhanced the company's awareness of the importance of actively injecting managerial resources to maintain fixed customers. For example, the company is making efforts to reduce disaffection among fixed customers by striving to improve service according to their requests via separate analysis of fixed customers' responses in room questionnaires and guest satisfaction surveys.

Non-fixed customers are divided into those likely or unlikely to become fixed customers in the future, and the company promotes further stays to those who may become fixed customers. As can be understood from the fact that the regression coefficient of the number of years of membership in Table 2 has a negative value for Segments 2–5, the higher the number of years of membership, the smaller the marginal profit by customer in 2015. In other words, it could be more efficient to undertake sales and promotion activity to encourage stays by customers who have been members for a short time and who currently only stay a few nights than to undertake such activities targeting non-fixed customers who are long-time Company A members.

To stabilize operating profit, in addition to transforming fixed costs into variable costs, it is necessary to create and maintain fixed customers. Company A operates luxury hotels, and so it is essential to maintain service quality and a luxury atmosphere, which makes it hard to replace fixed costs with variable costs by, for example, introducing automated check-in, rationalizing the range of services on offer, or utilizing casual staff. For a company like Company A, engaging in relationship marketing with the goal of creating good relationships with customers is an important measure to stabilize operating profit.

5. Conclusion

This study uses a Japanese hotel chain as a research site to test whether the stability of marginal profit attributable to fixed customers is higher than that attributable to non-fixed customers. The results show that the stability of fixed customers' marginal profit is higher. For companies like Company A, where it is difficult to transform fixed costs into variable costs, creating and maintaining fixed customers is important in efforts to stabilize operating profit.

There remain several limitations in this study and issues for future research. First, it is necessary to verify the difference in regression coefficients between segments statistically. Second, only the correlation of marginal profit by customers in two terms is verified in this study, and it would be helpful in the future to verify whether the marginal profit attributable to fixed customers is stable over multiple terms.

References

Bloom, N., Bond. S., and Reenen, J. V. 2007. Uncertainty and Investment Dynamics, *Review of Economic Studies*, 74(2), 391–415.

Dittman, D. A., Hesford, J. W., and Potter., G. 2009. Managerial Accounting in the Hospitality Industry. In Chapman, C. S., Hopwood, A. G., and Shields, M. D. (Eds.), *Handbook of Management Accounting Research*, Vol. 3, Elsevier, Amsterdam, pp. 353–1369,

Graham, J. R., Harvey, C. R., and Rajgopal, S. 2005. The Economic Implications of Corporate Financial Reporting, *Journal of Accounting and Economics*, 40, 3–73.

Gruca, T. S. and Rego, L. L. 2005. Customer Satisfaction, Cash Flow, and Shareholder Value, *Journal of Marketing*, 69, 115–130.

Komura, A. 2014. The Impact of Repurchase on the Stability of Transaction Amount: To Investigate the Relation between Customer Relationship and Sales Stability, *Studies in Business Administration (Meiji University)*, 41, 39–56 (In Japanese).

Komura, A. and Suzuki, K. 2014. The Effect of Customer Relationship on a Correlation between Past Sales and Future Sales: Based on the Data of Membership Customers of Company A, *The International Academy of Strategic Management*, 3(2), 161–172 (In Japanese).

Lev, B. 1974. On the Association between Operating Leverage and Risk, *The Journal of Financial and Quantitative Analysis*, 9(4), 627–641.

Lev, B. 1983. Some Economic Determinants of Timev Series Properties of Earnings, *Journal of Accounting and Economics*, 5, 31–48.

Li, S. and Richie, N. 2016. Income Smoothing and the Cost of Debt, China *Journal of Accounting Research*, 9 (3), 175–190.

Martinez, A. and Castro, M. 2011. Bond ratings and Income Smoothing in Brazil, *Latin American Business Review*, 12(2), 59–81.

Niimi, K. 2011. Positive Analysis of Variability and "Forecastability" of Recurring Profit, Considering the Relationship of Future Profit/Forecast Profit and Profit Variation, *Business and Economic Review*, 21(5), 40–63 (In Japanese).

Srivastava, R. K., Shervani, T. A., and Fahey, L. 1997. Driving Shareholder Value: The Role of Marketing in Reducing Vulnerability and Volatility of Cash Flows, *Journal of Market-Focused Management*, 2(1), 49–64.

Srivastava, R. K., Shervani, T. A., and Fahey, L. 1998. Market-Based Assets and Shareholder Value: A Framework for Analysis, *Journal of Marketing*, 62(January), 2–18.

Suzuki, K. 2005. An Evaluation Model of Profit Stability Based on the Concept of Fixed Revenue. *Bulletin of the Institute of Social Sciences, Meiji University,* 43(2), 163–174 (In Japanese).

Suzuki, K. 2007. A Consideration on the Applicability of Fixed Revenue Accounting. *The Accounting,* 171(2), 218–229 (In Japanese).

Suzuki, K., Matsumoto, Y., and Matsuoka, K. 2006. A Study on the Financial Effect of Revenue Fixation. *Accounting Progress,* 7, 46–58 (In Japanese).

Tarasi, C. O., Bolton, R. N., Gustafsson, A., and Walker, B. A. 2013. Relationship Characteristics and Cash Flow Variability: Implications for Satisfaction, Loyalty, and Customer Portfolio Management, *Journal of Service Research,* 16(2), 121–137.

Trueman, B. and Titman, S. 1988. An explanation for accounting income smoothing. *Journal of Accounting Research,* 26(Supplement), 127–139.

Part 3
Growth Analysis

Chapter 5

Variance Analysis in Fixed Revenue Accounting

Kohsuke Matsuoka

1. Introduction

On the basis of their relationship with a firm, customers can be segmented into four groups: New customers, fixed customers, non-fixed customers, and defectors. Measuring financial performance, such as the sales, costs, and profits of each customer segment, enables the firm to capture the connection between customer relationship and financial performance. Fixed revenue accounting (FRA) was proposed as a management accounting tool to relate customer relationship with financial performance (Suzuki, 2007).

However, customer relationships change over time: Customers are first acquired by the firm, then they go back and forth between fixed and non-fixed customers, and finally they become defectors if they feel dissatisfied with the firm's products or services. Changes in customer relationship bring about changes in financial performance, especially sales. Therefore, there is a close link between customer relationship and financial performance.

This chapter suggests a model to measure the impacts of new customer acquisition, fixed customer development, and customer defection on sales growth based on the FRA framework. In addition, a variance analysis model that relates sales variance to acquisition, development, and defection is presented with numerical examples. I call the model the "Bathtub Model variance analysis" (BMVA). I use the word "bathtub" because there is an analogy between customer relationship and water current in a bathtub. The Bathtub Model will be explained in detail later.

This chapter is structured as follows. I begin by introducing the Bathtub Model, which relates changes in customer relationship to sales growth based on the FRA framework (Matsuoka and Suzuki, 2009). I then propose change rates in the Bathtub Model. In the following section, I show how to calculate sales growth using the change rates. I then demonstrate the BMVA using numerical examples. After that, I discuss the difference between traditional variance analysis and the BMVA. In the final section of the chapter, I provide a summary and suggest avenues for future research.

2. The Bathtub Model

The Bathtub Model is based on the four customer segments used in FRA: New customers, fixed customers, non-fixed customers, and defectors. *New customers* are customers who started the first transaction with the firm in less than a given period of time in the past. When new customers keep their relationship with the firm for over a given period of time, they are considered fixed customers or non-fixed customers. *Fixed customers* are defined as customers who are highly probable to continue their relationship with the firm, whereas *non-fixed customers* are not highly probable to do so. The probability of keeping a relationship with the firm can be measured based on transaction measures such as purchase frequency, sales amount, the number of consecutive periods the customer makes transactions, and so on. *Defectors* are people who have not been making any transaction with the firm for over a certain period of time.

The Bathtub Model is a Markov chain model that shows how customers transit among the aforementioned four relationship segments (Fig. 1). The Bathtub Model includes "bathtub" in its name because customer acquisition and defection are analogous to water inflow and outflow from a bathtub, and because migration between fixed and non-fixed customers seems like a convection current of hot and cold water in a bathtub. The Bathtub Model uses acquisition and defection rates to estimate the customer base fluctuations and migration rates. The mathematical detail of the change rates will be provided later.

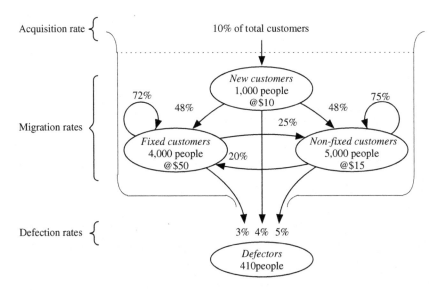

Acquisition rate

10% of total customers

Migration rates

72%   48%   New customers
1,000 people
@$10   48%   75%

25%

Fixed customers
4,000 people
@$50   20%   Non-fixed customers
5,000 people
@$15

Defection rates

3% 4% 5%

Defectors
410people

Fig. 1   Bathtub model.

Using the Bathtub Model enables managers to predict the three types of changes in customer quantity: The number of new customer acquisitions, customer migration between fixed and non-fixed customers, and customer defection. Multiplying sales per customer and these changes in customer quantity yields the amount of sales growth caused by customer acquisition, migration, and defection. Thus, the Bathtub Model is useful to split the impacts of changes in customer relationship on sales growth into three parts: acquisition effects, migration effects, and defection effects.

3. Change Rates

This section shows how to calculate customer quantity using three types of change rates: Acquisition, defection, and migration rates. For the sake of simplicity, the four customer segments are numbered as: New customers = 1; fixed customers = 2; non-fixed customers = 3; and defectors = 4. I assume that customers in segment 4 never make a transaction again and every customer belongs to one of each segment. Furthermore, let i denote the ith segment at time $t - 1$ and j denote the jth segment at time t. The number of customers is shown as $n_i(t - 1)$ for segment i at time $t - 1$ and $n_j(t)$ for segment j at time t. In addition, let me define $n_{ij}(t)$ as the number of customers in segment j at time t who transit from segment i at time $t - 1$.

The acquisition rate (a) and defection rate (d_i) affect the fluctuation of the customer base. a is the ratio of new customers (i.e., segment 1) at time t to customer base at time $t - 1$

$$a = \frac{n_1(t)}{\sum_{i=1}^{3} n_i(t-1)}. \tag{1}$$

Let me define a column vector for the number of new customers at time t as $n_1(t) = (n_1(t)\ 0\ 0)$, and a column vector for the number of customers in each segment at time $t - 1$ as $\mathbf{n}(t - 1) = (n_1(t - 1)\ n_2(t - 1)\ n_3(t - 1))$. $\mathbf{n}_1(t)$ is yielded by multiplying $\mathbf{n}(t - 1)$ by an acquisition rate matrix

$$\mathbf{A} = \begin{pmatrix} a & 0 & 0 \\ a & 0 & 0 \\ a & 0 & 0 \end{pmatrix}$$

$$\mathbf{n}_1(t) = \mathbf{n}(t - 1)\,\mathbf{A}, \tag{2}$$

d_i is the ratio of defectors (i.e., segment 4) from the ith segment at time t to customer population of the ith segment at time $t - 1$

$$d_i = \frac{n_{i4}(t)}{n_i(t-1)}. \tag{3}$$

Customers in segment 4 at time t from ith segment is written as $n_{i4}(t)$. Let $\mathbf{n}_4(t)$ be a column vector that has $n_{i4}(t)$ in its row elements; that is, $\mathbf{n}_4(t) = (n_{14}(t)\ n_{24}(t)\ n_{34}(t))$. $\mathbf{n}_4(t)$ can be produced by multiplying $\mathbf{n}(t - 1)$ by a defection rate matrix

$$\mathbf{D} = \begin{pmatrix} d_1 & 0 & 0 \\ 0 & d_2 & 0 \\ 0 & 0 & d_3 \end{pmatrix}$$

$$\mathbf{n}_4(t) = \mathbf{n}(t - 1)\,\mathbf{D}. \tag{4}$$

Migration rates (m_{ij}) denote migration to fixed customers or non-fixed customers. Customers at time $t - 1$ migrate to either fixed customers (i.e., segment 2) or non-fixed customers (i.e., segment 3) at time t unless they do not defect at time t. Therefore, m_{ij} shows the ratio of customers in segment 2 or 3 at time t to customers in segment i

$$m_{ij} = \frac{n_{ij}(t)}{n_i(t-1)}(i \neq 4, j \neq 1). \tag{5}$$

It should be noted that m_{i1}, the migration rate to segment 1, cannot be defined because any customer at time $t - 1$ never migrates to segment 1 at time t. In addition, m_{4j}, the migration rate from defectors, also cannot be defined because any customer in segment 4 is supposed never to start transactions again in any future.

Fixed customers and non-fixed customers at time t from segment i at time $t - 1$ are $n_2(t)$ and $n_3(t)$, respectively. Also, let me define a column vector for fixed customers as $\mathbf{n}_2(t) = (0\ n_2(t)\ 0)$ and a column vector for non-fixed customers as $\mathbf{n}_3(t) = (0\ 0\ n_3(t))$. Then, the sum of $\mathbf{n}_2(t)$ and $\mathbf{n}_3(t)$ is yielded by multiplying $\mathbf{n}(t - 1)$ by a migration rate matrix

$$\mathbf{M} = \begin{pmatrix} 0 & m_{12} & m_{13} \\ 0 & m_{22} & m_{23} \\ 0 & m_{32} & m_{33} \end{pmatrix}$$

$$\mathbf{n}_2(t) + \mathbf{n}_3(t) = \mathbf{n}(t - 1)\,\mathbf{M}. \tag{6}$$

Equation (6) shows the *levels* of fixed customers and non-fixed customers (segment 3) at time t rather than the *changes* from time $t - 1$ to time t. To capture the changes in the number of fixed customers and non-fixed customers, it is necessary to deduct the number of customers at time $t - 1$ from Eq. (6). As $\mathbf{n}(t - 1)\,\mathbf{M} - \mathbf{n}(t - 1) = \mathbf{n}(t - 1)\,(\mathbf{M} - \mathbf{I})$,

$$\mathbf{n}(t-1)(\mathbf{M} - \mathbf{I}) = \begin{pmatrix} n_1(t-1) \\ n_2(t-1) \\ n_3(t-1) \end{pmatrix}^{\mathrm{T}} \begin{pmatrix} -1 & m_{12} & m_{13} \\ 0 & m_{22}-1 & m_{23} \\ 0 & m_{32} & m_{33}-1 \end{pmatrix}. \tag{7}$$

where **I** is a unit matrix and the superscript T means transpose. In this chapter, column vectors are transposed where necessary for want of space. In terms of the purpose to measure the migration effects of fixed customers and non-fixed customers, Eq. (7) is still insufficient. The sum of m_{ij} is less than 1; that is, $\sum_{j=1}^{3} m_{ij} = 1 - d_i$. This is because m_{ij} shows migration to fixed customers and non-fixed customers and excludes transition to defectors. Therefore, the sum of each column in Eq. (7) is $\left(\sum_{j=1}^{3} m_{ij}\right) - 1 = -d_i$; that is, Eq. (7) is contaminated with the decrease in fixed customers and non-fixed customers caused by defection.

To extract pure migration effects, Eq. (4) should be added to Eq. (7); that is,

$$\mathbf{n}(t-1)\,(\mathbf{M}\!-\!\mathbf{I}) + \mathbf{n}(t-1)\,\mathbf{D} = \mathbf{n}(t-1)\,(\mathbf{M}+\mathbf{D}\!-\!\mathbf{I}), \tag{8}$$

and because $d_i - 1 = \sum_{j=1}^{3} m_{ij}$, the second term of the right-hand side in Eq. (8), $\mathbf{M} + \mathbf{D}\!-\!\mathbf{I}$, can be rewritten as

$$\mathbf{M}+\mathbf{D}-\mathbf{I} = \begin{pmatrix} d_1 - 1 & m_{12} & m_{13} \\ 0 & m_{22}+d_2-1 & m_{23} \\ 0 & m_{32} & m_{33}+d_3-1 \end{pmatrix},$$

$$= \begin{pmatrix} -(m_{12}+m_{13}) & m_{12} & m_{13} \\ 0 & -m_{23} & m_{23} \\ 0 & m_{32} & -m_{32} \end{pmatrix}.$$

The above matrix is considered a migration rate matrix before defection. Let me denote it by $\mathbf{M}^*$. Thus, migration before defection can be written as

$$\mathbf{n}_2(t) + \mathbf{n}_3(t) + \mathbf{n}_4(t) = \mathbf{n}(t)\,\mathbf{M}^*. \tag{9}$$

4 Sales Growth

In the previous section, I explained how to calculate the change in customer quantity for each segment at time t from customer quantity at time $t-1$

using acquisition rate, defection rate, and migration rate. To obtain sales growth caused by the changes in customer quantity, it is necessary to multiply only sales per customer and customer quantity changes. Let me define s_j as sales per customer for segment j at time t. Suppose that sales per customer for segment i at time $t - 1$, s_i, is the same as s_j if i equals j (i.e., $s_i = s_j$ for $i = j$). Let $\mathbf{S}$ be a sales per customer matrix; that is,

$$\mathbf{S} = \begin{pmatrix} s_1 & 0 & 0 \\ 0 & s_2 & 0 \\ 0 & 0 & s_3 \end{pmatrix}.$$

Let me begin with the impact of change in customer base, that is, acquisition effects and defection effects. The effect of acquisition on sales growth is denoted by $\mathbf{ae}(t)$, which is calculated by multiplying Eq. (2) by $\mathbf{S}$

$$\mathbf{ae}(t) = \mathbf{n}(t - 1) \, \mathbf{A} \, \mathbf{S}. \tag{10}$$

Defection effects on sales growth mean a decrease in sales caused by a shrinking customer base; that is, sales *negatively* grows when defection occurs. $\mathbf{de}(t)$ is a column vector for the effects of defection on negative sales growth at time t, which is produced by multiplying $\mathbf{S}$ by Eq. (4)

$$\mathbf{de}(t) = \mathbf{n}(t - 1) \, (-\mathbf{D}) \, \mathbf{S}. \tag{11}$$

The defection rate matrix $\mathbf{D}$, the second term of the right-hand side in Eq. (11) is negative as $\mathbf{de}_t$ means negative sales growth caused by a decrease in customer quantity.

Migration effects on sales growth are generated when customers at time $t - 1$ migrate to the fixed customer or non-fixed customer segment at time t. Let $\mathbf{me}(t)$ be a column vector for migration effects, which is calculated by multiplying Eq. (9) by $\mathbf{S}$

$$\mathbf{me}(t) = \mathbf{n}(t - 1) \, \mathbf{M}^* \, \mathbf{S}. \tag{12}$$

Suppose that customer quantity and sales per customer of each segment in Fig. 1 are the initial values at time 0. As is always assumed in Markov processes, probabilities in the Bathtub Model can be set as constant; that is, customer relationship changes at a constant rate. This assumption enables the firm to estimate the sales growth in the next period. Using the Bathtub Model, estimated sales growth at time 1 are separated into acquisition effects, defection effects, and migration effects as shown below

$$
\begin{pmatrix} 1,000 \\ 4,000 \\ 5,000 \end{pmatrix}^{\mathrm{T}}
\begin{pmatrix} 0.10 & 0 & 0 \\ 0.10 & 0 & 0 \\ 0.10 & 0 & 0 \end{pmatrix}
\begin{pmatrix} \$10 & 0 & 0 \\ 0 & \$50 & 0 \\ 0 & 0 & \$15 \end{pmatrix}
= \begin{pmatrix} \$10,000 \\ \$0 \\ \$0 \end{pmatrix}^{\mathrm{T}},
$$

$$
\begin{pmatrix} 1,000 \\ 4,000 \\ 5,000 \end{pmatrix}^{\mathrm{T}}
\begin{pmatrix} -0.04 & 0 & 0 \\ 0 & -0.03 & 0 \\ 0 & 0 & -0.05 \end{pmatrix}
\begin{pmatrix} \$10 & 0 & 0 \\ 0 & \$50 & 0 \\ 0 & 0 & \$15 \end{pmatrix}
= \begin{pmatrix} -400 \\ -6,000 \\ -3,750 \end{pmatrix}^{\mathrm{T}}, \text{and}
$$

$$
\begin{pmatrix} 1,000 \\ 4,000 \\ 5,000 \end{pmatrix}^{\mathrm{T}}
\begin{pmatrix} -0.96 & 0.48 & 0.48 \\ 0 & -0.25 & 0.25 \\ 0 & 0.20 & -0.20 \end{pmatrix}
\begin{pmatrix} \$10 & 0 & 0 \\ 0 & \$50 & 0 \\ 0 & 0 & \$15 \end{pmatrix}
= \begin{pmatrix} -\$9,600 \\ \$24,000 \\ \$7,200 \end{pmatrix}^{\mathrm{T}}.
$$

The sum of all the elements in each vector yields total estimated effects: $10,000 ($10,000 + $0 + $0) for acquisition effects, −$10,150 for defection effects (−$400 − $6,000 − $3,750), and $21,600 (−$9,600 + $24,000 + $7,200) for migration effects. Therefore, total estimated sales growth is $21,450 ($10,000 − $10,150 + $21,600).

5. Variance

As demonstrated above, the Bathtub Model helps managers estimate future sales growth on the assumption that acquisition, defection, and migration rates are constant over time. Panel A of Table 1 is a summary of estimated sales growth. In reality, various internal and external factors influence acquisition, defection, and migration rates. As a result, there would be a difference between *ex ante* change rates and *ex post* change rates that causes variance between estimated sales growth and actual sales growth. Hence, it is essential to analyze the variance and, if necessary, take action.

Table 1. Sales growth and variance.

	Total		New customers		Fixed customers		Non-fixed customers	
Panel A: Estimation								
Actual sales in time 0	$ 285,000		$ 10,000		$ 200,000		$ 75,000	
Estimated acquisition effect	10,000		10,000		—		—	
Estimated defection effects	−10,150		−400		−6,000		−3,750	
Estimated migration effects	21,600		−9,600		24,000		7,200	
Estimated sales growth	21,450		0		18,000		3,450	
Estimated sales in time 1	306,450		10,000		218,000		78,450	
Panel B: Actual results								
Actual sales in time 0	$ 285,000		$ 10,000		$ 200,000		$ 75,000	
Actual acquisition effect	8,000		8,000		—		—	
Actual defection effects	−6,450		−200		−4,000		−2,250	
Actual migration effects	27,300		−9,800		32,000		5,000	
Actual sales growth	28,850		−2,000		28,000		2,250	
Actual sales in time 1	313,850		8,000		228,000		77,850	
Panel C: Variance								
Estimated sales in time 1	$ 306,450		$ 10,000		$ 218,000		$ 78,450	
Acquisition variance	2,000	[U]	2,000	[U]	—		—	
Defection variance	3,700	[F]	200	[F]	2,000	[F]	1,500	[F]
Migration variance	5,700	[F]	−200	[U]	8,000	[F]	−2,100	[U]
Variance	7,400	[F]	2,000	[U]	10,000	[F]	600	[U]
Actual sales in time 1	313,850		8,000		228,000		77,850	

Panel B of Table 1 shows actual sales growth. To focus on variance caused by change rates fluctuations, let me suppose actual sales per customer for each segment is completely the same as the estimation; i.e., there is no variance caused by the difference between estimated and actual sales per customer. Substituting actual change rates for estimated change rates yields actual sales growth. Suppose that actual results of acquisition rate matrix $\mathbf{A}$, defection rate matrix $\mathbf{D}$, and migration before defection matrix $\mathbf{M}^*$ are, respectively,

$$\mathbf{A} = \begin{pmatrix} 0.08 & 0 & 0 \\ 0.08 & 0 & 0 \\ 0.08 & 0 & 0 \end{pmatrix}, \mathbf{D} = \begin{pmatrix} 0.02 & 0 & 0 \\ 0 & 0.02 & 0 \\ 0 & 0 & 0.03 \end{pmatrix}, \text{ and } \mathbf{M}^* = \begin{pmatrix} -0.98 & 0.50 & 0.48 \\ 0 & -0.25 & 0.25 \\ 0 & 0.22 & -0.22 \end{pmatrix}.$$

Therefore, actual acquisition effects, defection effects, and migration effects of sales growth are

$$\begin{pmatrix} 1,000 \\ 4,000 \\ 5,000 \end{pmatrix}^T \begin{pmatrix} 0.08 & 0 & 0 \\ 0.08 & 0 & 0 \\ 0.08 & 0 & 0 \end{pmatrix} \begin{pmatrix} \$10 & 0 & 0 \\ 0 & \$50 & 0 \\ 0 & 0 & \$15 \end{pmatrix} = \begin{pmatrix} \$8,000 \\ \$0 \\ \$0 \end{pmatrix}^T,$$

$$\begin{pmatrix} 1,000 \\ 4,000 \\ 5,000 \end{pmatrix}^T \begin{pmatrix} -0.02 & 0 & 0 \\ 0 & -0.02 & 0 \\ 0 & 0 & -0.03 \end{pmatrix} \begin{pmatrix} \$10 & 0 & 0 \\ 0 & \$50 & 0 \\ 0 & 0 & \$15 \end{pmatrix} = \begin{pmatrix} -\$200 \\ -\$4,000 \\ -\$2,250 \end{pmatrix}^T, \text{ and}$$

$$\begin{pmatrix} 1,000 \\ 4,000 \\ 5,000 \end{pmatrix}^T \begin{pmatrix} -0.98 & 0.50 & 0.48 \\ 0 & -0.25 & 0.25 \\ 0 & 0.22 & -0.22 \end{pmatrix} \begin{pmatrix} \$10 & 0 & 0 \\ 0 & \$50 & 0 \\ 0 & 0 & \$15 \end{pmatrix} = \begin{pmatrix} -\$9,800 \\ \$32,000 \\ \$5,100 \end{pmatrix}^T.$$

The sum of all the elements in each vector yields total actual effects: $8,000 ($8,000 + $0 + $0) for acquisition effects, −$6,450 for defection effects (−$200 − $4,000 − $2,250), and $27,300 (−$9,800 + $32,000 + $5,100) for migration effects. Therefore, total actual sales growth is $28,850 ($8,000 − $6,450 + $27,300).

Deducting estimated sales growth from actual sales growth yields variances (Panel C of Table 1). The acquisition variance, defection variance, and migration variance are

$$\begin{pmatrix} \$8,000 \\ \$0 \\ \$0 \end{pmatrix}^T - \begin{pmatrix} \$10,000 \\ \$0 \\ \$0 \end{pmatrix}^T = \begin{pmatrix} \$2,000[F] \\ \$0 \\ \$0 \end{pmatrix}^T,$$

$$\begin{pmatrix} -\$200 \\ -\$4,000 \\ -\$2,250 \end{pmatrix}^{\mathrm{T}} - \begin{pmatrix} -\$400 \\ -\$6,000 \\ -\$3,750 \end{pmatrix}^{\mathrm{T}} = \begin{pmatrix} \$200[F] \\ \$2,000[F] \\ \$1,500[F] \end{pmatrix}^{\mathrm{T}}, \text{ and}$$

$$\begin{pmatrix} -\$9,800 \\ \$32,000 \\ \$5,100 \end{pmatrix}^{\mathrm{T}} - \begin{pmatrix} -\$9,600 \\ \$24,000 \\ \$7,200 \end{pmatrix}^{\mathrm{T}} = \begin{pmatrix} \$200[U] \\ \$8,000[F] \\ \$2,100[U] \end{pmatrix}^{\mathrm{T}},$$

where [F] and [U], respectively, mean favorable and unfavorable. The sum of all the elements in each vector produces total variance: $2,000 [F] ($2,000 + $0 + $0) for acquisition variance, $3,700 [F] ($200 [F] + $2,000 [F] + $1,500 [F]) for defection variance, and $5,700 [F] for migration variance. Therefore, total variance is $7,400 [F] ($2,000 [U] + $3,700 [F] + $5,700 [F]).

Table 2 summarizes total estimated effects, total actual effects, and total variances for acquisition, defection, and migration. The results imply that the firm was successful in exceeding the estimated sales growth of $21,450 by $7,400. This was because although the firm could not achieve estimated new customer acquisition (total acquisition variance: $2,000 [U]), it was successful in exceeding the estimation of preventing customer defection (total defection variance: $3,700 [F]) and migrating customers to fixed customers (total migration variance: $5,700 [F]).

Needless to say, in reality, any of acquisition variance, defection variance, and migration variance would show unfavorable results. Actions the firm can take are to raise customer expectation through advertisement for

Table 2. Summary of variance.

	Total estimated sales growth (1)	Total actual sales growth (2)	Variance (3) = (2) − (1)	
Acquisition	$ 10,000	$ 8,000	$ 2,000	[U]
Defection	−10,150	−6,450	3,700	[F]
Migration	21,600	27,300	5,700	[F]
Total	21,450	28,850	7,400	[F]

customer acquisition, solve customer dissatisfaction through reinforce-
ment of complaint handling ability, and enhance customer loyalty through
enforcement of a frequency program for customer migration.

6. Discussion

6.1 *Calculation of variance*

The BMVA produces variance by comparing actual sales growth with
estimated sales growth. On the other hand, traditional variance analysis
calculates variance by comparing actual sales with estimated sales. Table 3
compares sales growth variance and sales variance. Suppose that actual
sales was $285,000 in time 0 and recall that the Bathtub Model esti-
mated sales growth at time 1 of $21,450. Then, the estimated sales in
time 1 would be $306,450 ($285,000 + $21,450). The actual sales
growth was $28,850; however, the actual sales at time 1 was $313,850
($285,000 + $28,850). Therefore, the sales variance is $7,400 [F]
($313,850 — $285,000), which is the same as the sales growth variance.
The difference between the BMVA and the traditional variance analysis
is whether the variance calculation includes sales in time 0 of $285,000
(Matsuoka and Hosoda, 2014).

The concept of revenue momentum explains the difference between the
BMVA and the traditional variance analysis. Revenue momentum is "the
tendency of revenues to recur" and is "due to a customer's tendency to go
back to the same seller in order to avoid an additional cost of getting
acquainted with a new seller" (Glover and Ijiri, 2002, p. 49). On the basis
of the concept of revenue momentum, sales of $285,000 in time 0 would
recur in time 1.

Table 3.   Calculation of variance.

	Estimation (1)	Actual results (2)	Variance (3) = (2) − (1)	
Sales in time 0	$ 285,000	$ 285,000	$ −	
Sales growth	21,450	28,850	7,400	[F]
Sales in time 1	306,450	313,850	7,400	[F]

The BMVA excludes existing revenue momentum, or sales in time 0, from performance evaluation at time 1 because just keeping a relationship with current customers would generate the same amount of sales in the next period. Considered contribution to performance is sales growth caused by promoting new customer acquisition and fixed customer development and by preventing current customer defection.

Traditional variance analysis assumes that there is no revenue momentum; that is, the firm earns sales from scratch every period. Under the circumstances, sales is considered the contribution to the firm's performance. If a company adopts this traditional view of performance, then it makes no sense of dividing sales in time 1 into sales in time 0 and sales growth. Therefore, variance is never related to sales growth.

Although both the BMVA and traditional variance analysis produce the same amount of total variance, the difference of whether current revenue momentum is included in variance calculation influences performance evaluation. The BMVA magnifies the impact of variance on performance evaluation compared with traditional variance analysis. For instance, in the BMVA, the variance indicates that the actual sales growth exceeded the estimation by around 34.5% ($7,400 ÷ $21,450). Therefore, the firm achieved an excellent performance. On the other hand, in the traditional variance analysis, the variance indicates that the actual sales showed a slight excess of 2.4% ($7,400 ÷ $306,450) to the estimated sales. Hence, the firm's performance was considered as expected.

Customer acquisition, customer defection, and customer migration cause changes in the customer relationship, which influences sales growth rather than sales. To evaluate outcomes from changes in customer relationship, the BMVA is more appropriate than traditional variance analysis.

6.2 *Breakdown of variance*

Variance can be divided into sales per customer variance and customer quantity variance. Change in customer quantity of each segment is determined by acquisition, defection, and migration. Hence, the BMVA divides customer quantity variance into the acquisition, defection, and migration variances. On the other hand, traditional variance analysis divides variance into sales price variance and sales quantity variance. Sales quantity variance is further separated into sales mix variance and sales volume variance. Finally, sales volume variance is composed of market share variance and market volume variance (Backer and Jacobsen, 1964, p. 491).

Although the variance breakdown in the BMVA seems quite different from traditional variance analysis, there is a similarity. Sales of the ith segment can be written as

$$
\begin{aligned}
\text{Sales}_i &= \text{Sales per customer}_i \times \text{Customer quantity}_i \\
&= \text{Sales price}_i \times \text{Sales quantity per customer}_i \times \text{Customer quantity}_i \\
&= \text{Sales price}_i \times \text{Sales quantity}_i.
\end{aligned}
$$

These equations imply that sales per customer variance is divided into sales price variance and sales quantity per customer variance, and the sum of sales quantity per customer variance and customer quantity variance is equal to sales quantity variance (Matsuoka and Suzuki, 2008). Furthermore, as stated above, the BMVA divides customer quantity variance into acquisition variance, defection variance, and migration variance. Hence, it seems reasonable to conclude that the BMVA is a method of analyzing the customer quantity variance part within sales quantity variance in terms of customer relationship change (Fig. 2).

Before continuing to the next section, there is one other thing that should be noted. Similar to sales mix variance and sales volume variance, customer quantity variance can be divided into customer mix variance and customer volume variance (Matsuoka and Suzuki, 2008). Customer mix of the ith segment means the distribution ratio of the customer

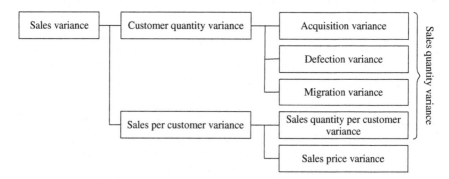

Fig. 2   Relation of the BMVA and traditional variance analysis.

quantity in the ith segment and customer volume is referred to as total customer quantity. However, this way of variance breakdown is problematic. The larger the mix of a fixed customer segment, the more favorable customer mix variance becomes. Increasing the number of fixed customers is one way to improve fixed customer mix. However, decreasing new customer acquisition and/or increasing defection from non-fixed customers also results in higher fixed customer mix. The BMVA introduced in this study should be used to evaluate whether a plan related to customer acquisition, customer defection, and customer migration is effectively implemented.

7. Summary and Future Research

This study presented the BMVA, which is a method to analyze sales growth variance in terms of customer relationship change. In comparison with traditional variance analysis, the BMVA has two features: First, it assumes that revenue has momentum caused by the relationship with current customers; second, it analyzes a part of sales quantity variance in terms of customer relationship change.

A possible future research direction is to establish a method to predict future sales growth on the basis of the Bathtub Model. As stated in Section 2, Markov processes, which are used to predict future states from the current states, lays the foundation of the Bathtub Model. Taking advantage of Markov processes, the BMVA estimates sales growth in the next period. The Bathtub Model is also useful to predict further regarding the future, and it even provides information on the convergent customer distribution and customer base growth rate. This information assists the firm in making decisions about how to balance resource allocation across new customer acquisition, current customer retention, and fixed customer development (Matsuoka, 2017).

Acknowledgment

This research was supported by Japan Society for the Promotion of Science (JSPS), Grant-in-Aid for Young Scientists (B), 2017–2019 (17K13825, Kohsuke Matsuoka).

References

Backer, B. and Jacobsen, L. E. 1964. *Cost Accounting: A Managerial Approach,* McGraw-Hill, New York, NY.

Glover, J. C. and Ijiri, Y. 2002. "Revenue Accounting" in the Age of E-Commerce: A Framework for Conceptual, Analytical, and Exchange Rate Considerations, *Journal of International Financial Management & Accounting,* 13(1), 32–72.

Suzuki, K. 2007. A Consideration on the Applicability of Fixed Revenue Accounting, *The Accounting,* 171(2), 46–57 (In Japanese).

Matsuoka, K. and Suzuki, K. 2008. Variance Analysis in Fixed Revenue Accounting: A Case Study of Customer Relationship Variance Analysis, *The Journal of Cost Accounting Research,* 32(1), 85–97 (In Japanese).

Matsuoka, K. and Suzuki, K. 2009. Variance Deployment based on the Bathtub Model Framework in Fixed Revenue Accounting, *The Journal of Cost Accounting Research,* 33(2), 45–58 (In Japanese).

Matsuoka, K. and Hosoda, M. 2014. Relationship between Bathtub Model Variance Analysis and Triple-Entry Bookkeeping, *Japanese Journal of Strategic Management,* 3(1), 93–108 (In Japanese).

Matsuoka, K. 2017. Evolving Markov Chain Model in Revenue Accounting. Proceedings of the Association of Asia Pacific Management Accounting Association 13th Annual Conference, China, Paper ID 30, 1–29 (USB).

Chapter 6

Bathtub Model Variance Analysis at a Japanese Hotel Chain

Kohsuke Matsuoka

1. Introduction

On the basis of customer relationships, fixed revenue accounting (FRA) measures and divides customers into four segments: New customers, fixed customers, non-fixed customers, and defectors. *New customers* are referred to as customers who started the first transaction with the firm in less than a given period of time in the past. When new customers keep their relationship with the firm over a given period of time, they are considered fixed or non-fixed customers. *Fixed customers* are defined as customers who are highly probable to continue their relationship with the firm; *non-fixed customers* are not highly probable to do so. The probability of keeping a relationship with the firm can be measured based on transaction measures such as purchase frequency, sales amount, the number of consecutive periods the customer makes transactions, and so on. *Defectors* are people who have not been making any transactions with the firm for a certain period of time. Measuring financial performance, such as sales for each segment, enables the firm to understand the financial impacts of customer relationship (Suzuki, 2007).

Customer relationship stochastically changes over time. Change processes can be modeled as a Markov chain model. The Markov chain model for depicting customer relationship change is called the *bathtub model* (Matsuoka and Suzuki, 2009). The bathtub model has three types of change rates: Acquisition rate of new customers, defection rate of defectors, and migration rate between fixed and non-fixed customers. On the basis of these change rates, the bathtub model estimates sales growth. Comparing the estimated sales growth and actual results yields variance. Thus, the bathtub model is applicable to variance analysis.

Matsuoka (2018) mathematically defines the *bathtub model variance analysis* (BMVA) and clarifies its difference from traditional variance analysis. However, he does not provide any practical significance of the BMVA. This chapter aims at exploring the practical implications through a case study at a Japanese hotel chain, hereinafter referred to as "Company A."

This study is organized as follows. I begin with a brief explanation of change rates and the BMVA. I then show the research design of the case study such as the hotel chain's background and the design of the BMVA. Following that, I describe the results of the BMVA using data from Company A and state its practical significance. In the final section, I summarize the chapter and suggest avenues for future research.

2. Bathtub Model Variance Analysis

2.1 *Change rates and variance analysis*

Sales is the product of customer quantity and sales per customer. Of the two, the bathtub model describes customer quantity on the basis of acquisition, defection, and migration rates.

The four customer segments are numbered as: New customers = 1; fixed customers = 2; non-fixed customers = 3; and defectors = 4. Suppose that customers in segment 4 never make a transaction again and each customer belongs to one of those segments. Let i denote the ith segment at time $t-1$, and j denote the jth segment at time t. Then, acquisition rate (a), defection rate (d_i), and migration rate (m_{ij}) are, respectively, defined as

$$a = \frac{n_1(t)}{\sum_{i=1}^{3} n_i(t-1)}$$

$$d_i = \frac{n_{i4}(t)}{n_i(t-1)}$$

$$m_{ij} = \frac{n_{ij}(t)}{n_i(t-1)} \left(i \neq 4, j \neq 1\right),$$

where $n_i(t-1)$ is the customer quantity of segment i at time $t-1$, $n_1(t)$ is the customer quantity of segment 1 at time t, $n_{i4}(t)$ is the customer quantity of segment 4 who defected from segment i at time $t-1$, and $n_{ij}(t)$ is the customer quantity of segment j at time t who transited from segment i at time $t-1$.

It should be noted that m_{i1}, the migration rate to new customers, cannot be defined because any customer at time $t-1$ never migrates to segment 1 at time t. In addition, suppose defectors at time $t-1$ never start any transactions again in future. Therefore, m_{4j}, the migration rate from defectors, also cannot be defined.

Using these change rates, the BMVA breaks down customer quantity variance into acquisition variance, defection variance, and migration variance. The procedure can be summarized as follows. First, on the basis of a, d_i, and m_{ij}, the BMVA estimates change in customer quantity of new customers, defectors, fixed customers, and non-fixed customers. Second, the BMVA makes estimates of sales growth by multiplying the change in customer quantity by sales per customer. Finally, comparing the estimated sales growth with actual results, variance is calculated. Matsuoka (2017a) provides details about the BMVA.

2.2 *Difference from traditional variance analysis*

Compared with traditional variance analysis, the BMVA is characterized in two respects. First, the BMVA calculates variance comparing estimate and actual results of *sales growth* rather than *sales* (Matsuoka and Hosoda, 2014). Customer acquisition, defection, and migration changes customer relationship and eventually causes sales growth. As such, focusing on sales growth enables the firm to evaluate the financial impact of customer relationship change.

Second, customer quantity variance in the BMVA is a part of sales quantity variance in traditional variance analysis (Matsuoka and Suzuki, 2008). Sales quantity is the product of sales quantity per customer (sales quantity ÷ customer quantity) and customer quantity. Hence, sales quantity variance can be divided into sales quantity per customer variance and customer quantity variance. The BMVA breaks down customer quantity variance into acquisition variance, defection variance, and migration variance. Therefore, it can be said that the BMVA analyzes the customer

quantity part within sales quantity variance in terms of customer relationship change.

3. Research Design

3.1 Research site

Company A is a Japanese hotel chain and is suitable for the case study of
the BMVA model for two reasons. First, hotels generally have marketing
programs for acquiring new customers, preventing defectors, and developing fixed customers in place. Because hotels maintain large facilities and
many employees, fixed costs occupy a large part of total costs. Furthermore,
today's guest rooms cannot be sold tomorrow as they are perishable. Thus,
it is highly important for hotel companies to secure fixed customers and
revenues. The more fixed customers the hotel chain develops, the more
stable the hotel occupancy rate becomes.

Second, customer transaction data, which are necessary for the FRA to
segment customers, are available in hotels. Many hotels have an established customer relationship system, and Company A is no exception: it
has a membership system and collects customer transaction data.

3.2 Data

Japan's fiscal year starts in April and ends in March. The data for this case
study were customer transaction data in FY2005–FY2007. These data are
suitable for the purpose of exploring the practical significance of the
BMVA. Firms' financial performance is affected not only by internal but
also by external factors. Figure 1 shows Japan's real GDP from FY2003
to FY2012. The Japanese economy has grown steadily from FY2005 to
FY2007, implying that there had been no substantial external shocks.

On the other hand, since FY2008, the Japanese economy has been suf-
fering from huge external shocks: For example, the global financial crisis
knocked the Japanese economy in September 2008 and the Great East
Japan Earthquake in March 2011. Therefore, it is difficult to correctly
interpret Company A's internal efforts for acquiring new customers, preventing defectors, and developing fixed customers from customer transaction data since FY2008.

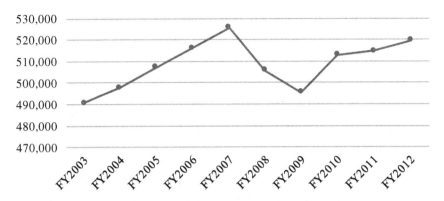

Fig. 1   Real gross domestic product of Japan (in billion JPY).
Source: The data are collected from National Accounts for 2015 (Cabinet Office, Government of Japan, 2017).

After showing the results of the BMVA, I will describe the discussion that Company A conducted about the results of the BMVA in the first half of FY2008, just before the global financial crisis. The objective of variance analysis is to promote organizational learning by clarifying the causes of variance (Horngren *et al.*, 2014, p. 266). Thus, focusing on the discussion is suitable for the purpose of this study. The discussion and actions made in or after the last half of FY2008 are excluded in this study as Company A struggled to deal with the turbulent economic environment.

3.3 *Customer segments*

Company A identifies new customers and defectors in terms of the presence or absence of registration to its membership system: New customers are customers who joined the membership system in the fiscal year; defectors are customers who quit the membership system in the fiscal year. It should be noted that new customers who quit the membership system in the same fiscal year are considered defectors.

Other customers are segmented into fixed customers and non-fixed customers: Fixed customers are referred to as customers who visited Company A's hotels six times or more in the fiscal year; non-fixed customers are defined as customers who visited the hotels five times or less in the fiscal year. This criterion is a rule of thumb at Company A. However, although the population of fixed customers was around 30% in FY2007, they contributed nearly 70% of total revenues. As these ratios are approximately corresponding to the well-known Pareto principle, it cannot be said that Company A's criterion is entirely wrong. Furthermore, using accustomed criteria enables Company A's managers to smoothly understand the information from the BMVA. Therefore, I adopt this criteria as it is.

3.4 Estimate of change rates and sales per customer

This study uses the data of FY2007 as actual results. The problem is how to estimate change rates and sales per customer to estimate sales growth.

I use actual change rates from FY2005 to FY2006 as estimated change rates in FY2007. As Fig. 1 shows, the Japanese economy from FY2005 to FY2007 remained stable. Therefore, it was rational to estimate that in FY2007, Company A would achieve new customer acquisition, defector prevention, and fixed customer development at the same rates as the actual rates from FY2005 to FY2006.

Actual sales per customer of FY2006 is used to estimate sales per customer for FY2007. However, as new customers join the membership system at some point in a fiscal year, sales per customer of new customers depends on when they join the membership. Then, I divide sales per customer of total customers in FY2006 by two and adopt the quotient as the estimated sales per customer of FY2007. The reason why I use the quotient is because new customers were assumed to join the membership randomly in the fiscal year.

It may not be appropriate for the actual sales per customer of FY2006 to be used as the estimate of FY2007. This is because it was probable that consumers' inclination to spend was picking up as the Japanese economy was rising in FY2006 and FY2007. However, the focus of this study is on customer quantity variance. Therefore, I only use the actual sales per customer of FY2006 as the estimate of FY2007.

3.5 Customer quantity flexible budget

It is well known among management accountants that deducting the static from the flexible budget produces sales quantity variance. In the same way, customer quantity variance can be calculated when the flexible budget is the product of estimated sales per customer and actual customer quantity. This flexible budget can be called the "customer quantity flexible budget."

Although deducting customer quantity flexible budget from actual sales yields sales per customer variance, this study does not go to that extent as the focus is on customer quantity variance.

3.6 Sales from defectors

Some defectors generate sales before quitting their membership at some point in a fiscal year. An increase in defections means more sales from defectors, generating favorable variance. Hence, this study excludes sales in the defector segment from variance analysis. Sales from defectors at Company A occupied only several percent of total sales in FY2007. Thus, excluding defector sales does not matter to the interpretation of the BMVA.

4. Results

4.1 Results of traditional variance analysis

Before showing the results of the BMVA, let me discuss sales quantity of the traditional variance analysis (Table 1). Because Company A operates hotels, sales quantity in this study means rooms sold. The sales quantity variance is calculated by deducting the static budget from the "sales quantity flexible budget," which is the product of the actual sales quantity and the estimated sales price. It should be noted that to protect confidentiality, the results in this study are adjusted within the extent to which the adjustment does not distort the interpretation.

Table 1 indicates that the company exceeded the estimated sales of ¥8,300 million by around 10.5% (872 ÷ 8,300). However, Table 1 does not separate the estimated sales in FY2007 into the actual sales in FY2006

Table 1.   Results of traditional variance analysis (in million JPY).

	Estimate (1)	Sales quantity flexible buget (2)	Sales quantity variance (3) = (2) −(1)	
Sales in FY2007	¥ 8,300	¥ 9,173	¥ 873	[F]

and the actual sales growth achieved in FY2007. Hence, it is impossible to evaluate the extent to which Company A achieved the estimated sales growth in FY2007.

Furthermore, Table 1 is not useful to relate the causes of favorable sales quantity variance to marketing programs; that is, it does not provide any information on new customer acquisition, defector prevention, and fixed customer development. Even if sales quantity variance is broken down into sales mix variance and sales volume variance, the information has little usefulness in evaluating the performance of marketing programs for building customer relationship. Needless to say, even if sales volume variance is further divided into market share variance and market volume variance, the same is true.

4.2 Results of the BMVA

As stated in Section 2, sales quantity variance is the sum of customer quantity variance and quantity per customer variance.[1] As is summarized in Table 2, the BMVA further divided customer quantity variance into acquisition, defection, and migration variance. The complete results for each customer segment are shown in the Appendix.

Each row of Table 2 indicates the effects of acquisition, defection, and migration on sales growth. First, the estimated sales growth in FY2007 was ¥502 million, and its breakdown was acquisition effects of ¥727 million, defection effects of –¥462 million, and migration effects of ¥237 million. The results imply that new customer acquisition was expected to be the most influential driver of Company A's sales growth.

Second, the customer quantity flexible budget of FY2007 was ¥896 million. The breakdown was acquisition effects of ¥507 million, defection effects of –¥431 million, and migration effects of ¥802 million. The results indicate that, in reality, the most influential driver of sales growth was the migration to fixed customers.

Finally, the customer quantity variance column of Table 2 shows that the customer quantity variance was ¥394 million [F] (896–502); that is,

---

[1]At Company A, sales quantity variance of ¥872 million [F] was divided into customer quantity variance of ¥394 million [F] and quantity per customer variance ¥478 million [F].

Table 2.   Summary of customer quantity variance (in million JPY).

	Estimate (1)	Customer quantity flexible buget (2)	Customer quantity variance (3) = (2) − (1)	
Sales in FY2006	¥ 8,300	¥ 8,300	¥ −	
Acquisition	727	507	219	[U]
Defection	−462	−431	30	[F]
Migration	237	820	583	[F]
Sales growth	502	896	394	[F]
Sales in FY2007	8,802	9,197	394	[F]

Company A's actual sales growth exceeded the estimate by around 78.5% (394 ÷ 502).

Breaking down the customer quantity variance into acquisition, defection, and migration variance makes it possible to evaluate which kind of customer relationship change caused the customer quantity variance. The acquisition variance was ¥219 million [U]; that is, Company A failed to achieve the estimated customer acquisition by around 30.1% (219 ÷ 727). The results imply that the ability of Company A to acquire new customers deteriorated.

The defection variance of ¥30 million [F] clarifies that Company A was slightly successful in preventing defectors by around 6.5% (30 ÷ 462) compared with the estimate. Thus, the estimates of defection effects were roughly as expected.

The migration variance of ¥583 million [F] implies that Company A far exceeded the estimated migration effects by around 246.0% (583 ÷ 237). Therefore, it can be safely said that Company A was very much successful in increasing fixed customers through marketing programs for customer satisfaction such as service quality improvement.

4.3 *Company A's reactions*

Following the results of the BMVA, managers at Company A learned about their marketing programs. First, they understood why the sales growth achieved much greater sales growth than the estimate. The achievement was mainly due to the success of fixed customer development. However, they also learned that they failed to acquire new customers as estimated. Therefore, they recognized that a revision of the current marketing programs for new customer acquisition would be necessary.

Second, the combination of successful fixed customer development and disappointing new customer acquisition interested managers because it signals that Company A's business has started to mature. The managers reached the consensus that Company A would need to invest in developing brand new hotels and searching for new target customer segments in order to secure further sales growth in the long term.

5. Discussion

As stated in Section 2, the BMVA is *theoretically* different from traditional variance analysis in two respects: first, the BMVA calculates sales growth variance rather than sales variance; second, the sales growth variance is divided into acquisition variance, defection variance, and migration variance. These characteristics enable the BMVA to evaluate the financial impacts of customer relationship change.

Through the case study, it is confirmed that these characteristics lead to at least two significant *practical* implications. First, performance evaluation and learning about marketing programs for changing customer relationship are made with high precision. In the case study of Company A, the unfavorable acquisition variance showed the corrosion of the sales force and/or hotel appeal to prospects; the insubstantially favorable defection variance implicated that the efforts to resolve customer dissatisfaction, such as improved complaint handling, were working as expected[2];

---

[2]Hotels deal with services rather than products. *Variability* is one of the service characteristics compared with products. Service quality always varies because it is determined by the interactions between customers and employees on a moment-to-moment basis. As a result, it is impossible to prevent all customers from being dissatisfied with the service. Therefore, "resolving customer complaints is a critical component of customer retention" (Kotler *et al.*, 2010, p. 42). To have effective complaint resolution, it is highly necessary for the firm to enhance the ability of service recovery. For instance, empowerment enables employees to resolve customer complaints. Another example is to give customers a chance to complain through customer hotlines, customer comment cards,

and the favorable migration variance indicated successful efforts to improve customer satisfaction. These variances identify the marketing efforts to be commended and the ones to be improved.

Second, combining the acquisition, defection, and migration variances allowed to consider information about the business lifecycle. The meaning of sales growth could be different depending on which marketing program for building customer relationship contributes to sales growth. Company A's managers considered that the combination of unfavorable acquisition variance and favorable migration variance implied their business life cycle would move forward to the mature phase. Then, the managers developed a critical feeling of their business losing growth in the long term. The sense of this crisis made them consider the development of hotels with new features and search for new target customer segments. Thus, the BMVA might promote decision-making in accordance with business life cycle.

6. Conclusion

This study described the case of Company A, which operates a hotel chain in Japan, to explore the practical significance of the BMVA. The case study showed that the BMVA promotes performance evaluation and learning of marketing programs for building customer relationship with high precision as it divides sales growth variance into acquisition, defection, and migration variances. In addition, the case study also implied that the BMVA might promote decision-making in accordance with business life cycle given the combination of acquisition, defection, and migration variances.

This study deals with only a single case study. Therefore, generalization of the implications in this study should be avoided. However, to confirm the practical significance of this new management accounting tool, there is no other way than observing it on a case-by-case basis. Hence, the future research avenue is to apply the BMVA to other firms.

---

and so on. Most customers just leave and never come back without making any complaint even though they feel dissatisfied.

K. Matsuoka

Appendix

Table A.1 shows the results of the BMVA by each segment. Let me focus on Panel C of Table A.1. The sales growth variance of new customer was ¥214 million [U] mainly due to the unfavorable acquisition variance of ¥219 million [U]. In the fixed customer segment, the sales growth variance of ¥723 million [F] was caused mainly by favorable migration variance of ¥712 million [F]. Finally, the sales growth variance of ¥114 million [U] in the non-fixed customer segment was mainly because of the unfavorable defection variance of ¥128 million [U].

Table A.1. Details of the BMVA (in million JPY).

	Total	New customers	Fixed customers	Non-fixed customers
Panel A: Estimate				
Actual sales in 2006	¥ 8,300	¥ 587	¥ 5,676	¥ 2,037
Estimated acquisition effect	727	727	–	–
Estimated defection effects	−462	−42	−291	−128
Estimated migration effects	237	−544	434	347
Estimated Sales growth	502	140	143	218
Estimated sales in 2007	8,802	727	5,820	2,255
Panel B: Customer quantity flexible budget				
Actual sales in FY2006	¥ 8,300	¥ 587	¥ 5,676	¥ 2,037
Actual acquisition effect	507	507	–	–
Actual defection effects	−431	−37	−279	−115
Actual migration effects	820	−544	1,146	219
Actual sales growth	896	−74	866	104
Customer quantity flexible budget	9,197	513	6,543	2,141

(Continued)

Table A.1. *(Continued)*

	Total		New customers		Fixed customers		Non-fixed customers	
Panel C: Customer quantity variance								
Estimated sales in FY2007	¥ 8,802		¥ 727		¥ 5,820		¥ 2,255	
Acquisition variance	219	[U]	219	[U]	–		–	
Defection variance	30	[F]	5	[F]	11	[F]	14	[F]
migration variance	583	[F]	–		712	[F]	128	[U]
Customer quantity variance	394	[F]	214	[U]	723	[F]	114	[U]
Customer quantity flexible budget	9,197		513		6,543		2,141	

Acknowledgment

The case study uses the same data as the one used in Matsuoka and Suzuki's study (2009). However, most of the results and interpretation are rewritten. I appreciate the Japanese Cost Accounting Association allowing me to edit the previously published case study.

This research was supported by Japan Society for the Promotion of Science (JSPS), Grant-in-Aid for Young Scientists (B), 2017–2019 (17K13825, Kohsuke Matsuoka).

References

Cabinet Office, Government of Japan. p2017. *National Accounts for 2015*. Retrieved Mar 18, 2017. (2008SNA, benchmark year = 2011). Available at http://www.esri.cao.go.jp/jp/sna/data/data_list/kakuhou/files/h26/tables/26ffm1rn_jp.xls.

Horngren, C. T., Datar, S. M., and Rajan, M. V. 2014. *Cost Accounting: A Managerial Emphasis*, 15th edition, Hall NJ: Pearson Prentice.

Kotler, P., Bowen, J. T., and Makens, J. C. 2010. *Marketing for Hospitality and Tourism*, 15th Edition, Pearson Prentice Hall, NJ.

Matsuoka, K. and Suzuki, K. 2008. Variance Analysis in Fixed Revenue Accounting: A Case Study of Customer Relationship Variance Analysis, *The Journal of Cost Accounting Research*, 32(1), 85–97 (In Japanese).

Matsuoka, K. and Suzuki, K. 2009. Variance Deployment Based on the Bathtub Model Framework in Fixed Revenue Accounting, *The Journal of Cost Accounting Research*, 33(2), 45–58 (In Japanese).

Matsuoka, K. and Hosoda, M. 2014. Relationship between Bathtub Model Variance Analysis and Triple-Entry Bookkeeping, *Japanese Journal of Strategic Management*, 3(1), 93–108 (In Japanese).

Matsuoka, K. 2018. Variance Analysis in Fixed Revenue Accounting, *Japanese Management and International Studies*, 15, 97–112.

Suzuki, K. 2007. A Consideration on the Applicability of Fixed Revenue Accounting, *The Accounting*, 171(2), 46–57 (In Japanese).

Chapter 7

Promoting and Hindering Factors in the Introduction of Fixed Revenue Accounting: A Case Study in a B2B Company Based on Management Accounting Change

Masahiro Hosoda, Yoshitaka Myochin,
and Daisuke Tomita

1. Introduction

In recent years, companies have been searching for management accounting systems that best deal with the changing environment around them. Many use traditional management accounting systems like budget management alongside innovative management accounting systems such as Activity-Based Costing (ABC) and Balanced Scorecard (BSC) (e.g., Burns and Vaivio, 2001; Scapens *et al.*, 1996). Libby and Waterhouse (1996) and Williams and Seaman (2001) also demonstrated that many companies are engaged in such changes in management accounting systems and business practices. Management accounting change research is a stream that attempts to explain the factors behind these changes and the processes.

Management accounting change studies identify why and how management accounting systems and business practices are disseminated, introduced, changed, and refused. Many frameworks of this study were developed in Europe and North America (Yoshida, 2003). In this context, the factors that promote and hinder changes in management accounting systems were identified by applying the structural perspective (e.g., Cobb *et al.*, 1995; Innes and Mitchell, 1990; Kasurinen, 2002).

Applying a structural perspective consists of determining the relationship between the factors that promote and hinder elements and operations that cause changes in management accounting, based on variables discussed in contingency theory. There are both qualitative and quantitative approaches (Cobb *et al.*, 1995; Innes and Mitchell, 1990; Kasurinen, 2002; Libby and Waterhouse, 1996; Williams and Seaman, 2001).[1]

In the discussion of the changes in management accounting systems, the concept of fixed revenue accounting (FRA) was proposed in 2005. FRA is a "management control system that uses a model that measures the degree of influence the relationship of a company with its customers exerts on its financial performance to stimulate the implementation of relationship marketing strategies" (Suzuki, 2012, p. 24). Previous studies demonstrated practical applications of FRA (Suzuki, 2007) and variance analysis of FRA (Matsuoka and Suzuki, 2008, 2009).

However, no study thus far has attempted to explain the factors that promote or hinder the introduction of FRA from the perspective of management accounting change. For this reason, we thought it would be meaningful to explain these factors based on the qualitative approach by Cobb *et al.* (1995) and Innes and Mitchell (1990). We believe that we can provide useful knowledge to companies considering introducing FRA in terms of when they can do so.

Therefore, this paper relies on Cobb *et al.* (1995) and Innes and Mitchell (1990) to identify the factors that promote or hinder the introduction of FRA through a case study in a business to business (B2B) company.[2]

---

[1]Both external and internal factors influence the design of management control systems (company size, environment, technology, mutual relationship, strategy) (Anthony and Govindarajan, 2007, p. 576). Contingency theory does not discuss how these variables influence the dynamic aspect of management accounting systems, which acquire company-and-industry-specific formats (Innes and Mitchell, 1990). This began a discussion on the structural perspective by Innes and Mitchell (1990) and others.

[2]This paper was based on a case study to demonstrate the change process until the introduction of FRA. We believed that it would be effective to use the qualitative framework

The structure of this paper is as follows: the Section 2 provides an overview on previous studies, and Section 3 explains the research design. Section 4 presents the research results, which we discuss in Section 5. The final section discusses the conclusion, significance, and the future research task of this paper.

2. Factors that Promote or Hinder Changes in Management Accounting

Innes and Mitchell (1990) proposed one of the main theories about the factors and operations that promote or hinder changes in management accounting. After conducting a case study of seven electronic equipment manufacturers in Scotland, Innes and Mitchell (1990) cited three factors of change in accounting systems: motivators, catalysts, and facilitators.

Motivators are factors that indirectly promote changes in management accounting such as changes in the competitive environment and production technology. Catalysts are factors that directly promote management accounting change such as a decline in market share and profitability. Facilitators are elements such as adequate accounting staff and information systems, which are not sufficient by themselves, but necessary for supporting management accounting changes (Innes and Mitchell, 1990). With regard to the relationship of these three factors, Innes and Mitchell (1990) stated that motivators and catalysts promote management accounting changes, however they are only effective with the presence of facilitators.

In a later study, relying on Innes and Mitchell (1990), Cobb *et al.* (1995) added three new factors to the existing motivators, catalysts, and facilitators: leadership, momentum to continue the change, and barriers to changes.

According to Cobb *et al.* (1995), the relationship between the three additional factors is as follows: barriers to management accounting changes are

---

of the structural perspective proposed by Cobb *et al.* (1995) and Innes and Mitchell (1990) to identify the kind of environment, the factors that promoted its introduction, and how the hindering factors work.

factors that either cause delay or hinder changes such as resistance from managers, change in accounting personnel, and lower awareness. Leadership and momentum to make the management accounting change sustainable are the two factors necessary to overcome these barriers.

In the case study of Cobb *et al.* (1995), the organization members acting as catalysts to promote changes to the management accounting exerted the leadership. As momentum that would sustain the management accounting changes, they explain that the company introduced, operated, improved, and repealed management accounting systems such as cost allocation and ABC repeatedly under the expectation of a sustainable change in the entire organization.

This demonstrates that motivators, catalysts, facilitators, momentum for change, and leadership are important factors that promote changes to management accounting systems (Innes and Mitchell, 1990). In addition, overcoming barriers to changes requires leadership and momentum to sustain the changes in management accounting (Cobb *et al.*, 1995).

Therefore, through a case study in Company A, this study will identify the factors that promote or hinder the introduction of FRA based on the qualitative approach by Cobb *et al.* (1995) and Innes and Mitchell (1990).

3. Research Design

3.1 *Research method*

This study utilizes a case study as a research method. A case study aims to investigate a contemporary phenomenon that occur in a real-world context using multiple source of evidence (Yin, 2014).

In order to obtain the data we use in our case study, we conducted research in various ways. More specifically, we conducted continuous non-structural interviews related to the objective and results of the introduction of FRA between 2009 and 2014, and the authors participated in the project to introduce variance analysis based on Company A's FRA between 2009 and 2011. The collected data includes interviews and records of observations, internal files offered by the company, and publications on Company A. To remove researchers' bias from the obtained results, we created cases and reports and had them verified by the president and executive sales director.

3.2 *Research site*

Company A is a B2B organization. Company A sells Company B's products to other companies as its main product. It expanded its businesses in recent years by establishing a department that designs and develops electronic components, and it started designing, manufacturing, and selling electronic components. During the research period, Company A had a capital stock of approximately $90,000.

We chose Company A because it newly introduced FRA and it continues to function. We believe that by setting Company A as our research site, we can identify the key factors for the introduction of FRA.

4. Results

This section presents the results of the case study in terms of the aforementioned six factors of management accounting change: (1) motivators, (2) catalysts, (3) facilitators, (4) leadership, (5) momentum for change, and (6) barriers to change (Fig. 1).

4.1 *Motivators*

Motivators are factors that indirectly promote changes in management accounting. According to the president of Company A, the electronic components industry has excessive competition on a global scale. Technologically inferior products were especially exposed to a cost offensive from low-cost imitation products from developing countries.

4.2 *Catalysts*

The motivators described above led to the decline in the price of products, which in turn resulted in a sharp decrease in the commercial profit rate, and this had a considerable impact on Company A's financials.

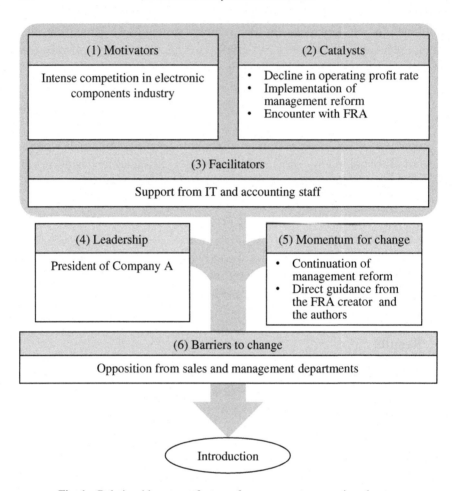

Fig. 1　Relationship among factors of management accounting change.
Source: Created by the authors based on Cobb *et al.* (1995).

Subsequently, in 2004, the president of Company A initiated management reform. As part of that process, a customer-oriented management philosophy and vision were formulated, and the company started showing a strong customer-oriented attitude. However, Company A had not yet developed a mechanism that could show how the results of the reform were reflected in the customer relationships, and how it impacted the company's financials. In these circumstances, FRA that could measure and evaluate how the customer relationships impacted a company's financials was devised at the same time, and the president coincidentally met the creator of FRA.

Therefore, the combination of the 2004 management reform following the decline in the commercial profit rate and the encounter with FRA worked as a catalyst for Company A, and thus the FRA introduction moved forward.

4.3 *Facilitators*

Even with factors that promote changes to management accounting, both direct (catalysts) and indirect (motivators), changes do not materialize without the support of accounting and IT staff.

In Company A, after proposing the management reform, the accounting and IT staff that endorsed the management reform helped improvement of the internal business systems for quality control and environmental management. They also gave all the necessary support to make it possible to analyze purchased products (price and volume) and date of sale by customer, so customers could be classified into segments prior to introducing FRA. Thus, the existence of IT staff and accounting staff promoted management accounting change as a facilitator.

4.4 *Leadership*

The presence of the aforementioned factors that directly or indirectly bring changes to management accounting are not sufficient for change to occur. When a barrier to change appears, without strong leadership from the senior members, there is a risk that resistance cannot be overcome, which will ultimately increase the risk of failure in attempting to change the management accounting system.

In the case of Company A, despite resistance from sales and management departments, the president exhibited strong leadership and went through with the management reform. The sales department was full of conceit about having the relationship with the main suppliers and even did not visit their customers. In addition, the management department was sluggish in its daily activities. Despite being a company that totally depended on its customers, it had a low-level awareness of its customers. Therefore, to implement the management reform, the president dedicated himself to improving the employees' awareness and spurring them on day and night.

4.5 *Momentum for change*

When a barrier appears, in addition to strong leadership, as discussed above, alongside momentum for change, which is a series of factors that sustain changes, the management accounting system can be successfully changed.

In Company A, the fact that the management reform continued despite opposition from employees, as well as the direct guidance from the creator of FRA, can be cited as examples of momentum for change.

As previously mentioned, FRA was devised while the president of Company A initiated the management reform. Then, while implementing the management reform, which consisted of modifying the organizational structure and formulating a management philosophy and vision, the company introduced FRA in 2007 under direct guidance from its creator. With FRA, it is possible to implement a management strategy drafted from the perspective of customers and accounting, and based on the company's philosophy and vision. It turned out to be exactly the management control system the president of Company A was seeking, in that it could convey managers' intentions to employees. In fact, Company A decided to use the profit and loss statement form of FRA (Fig. 2) to calculate its fixed operating profit.[3]

In addition, since it is not possible to evaluate the success of Company A's marketing strategy with the fixed operating profit figures alone properly, the Bathtub Model variance analysis (BMVA) was introduced in 2008 under the direct guidance of the authors. Table 1 shows the results of the BMVA ($t - 1$ and t periods). Additionally, each variance of t period

---

[3]Fixed operating profit is calculated by subtracting the segment common cost (fixed cost) from the contribution margin obtained from fixed customers.

April 1, 2011 - March 31, 2012

Item	Classification	Product Details	Total	Variable Customer	Semi-Fixed Customer	Fixed Customer
Sales	Product Series A					
	Product Series B					
	Product Series C					
	Product Series D					
	Total					
Direct Segment Cost (Variable)	Cost of Sales					
	Selling, general, and administrative expenses					
	Total					
	Marginal Profit					
Direct Segment Cost (Fixed)	Cost of Sales					
	Selling, general, and administrative expenses					
	Total					
	Contribution Margin					
Segment Common Cost (Fixed)	Cost of Sales					
	Selling, general, and administrative expenses 1					
	Selling, general, and administrative expenses 2					
	Total		(b)			
	Operating Income					
	Fixed Operating Profit			(a)		

Fig. 2 Profit and loss statement in the profit plan.

Note:*Fixed operating profit = (a) − (b).

Table 1.　Results of the BMVA.

(Unit: $10)			t-1 period	t period
Acquisition Variance			248,943	285,530
Defection Variance			▲ 275,687	▲ 281,778
	New Customers		▲ 48,042	▲ 109,819
	Variable Customers		▲ 88,792	▲ 32,103
	Semi-Fixed Customers		▲ 66,469	▲ 70,570
	Fixed Customers		▲ 72,384	▲ 69,286
Transition Variance			1,112,668	323,803
	New Customers		259,773	330,574
		New Customers	▲ 48,042	▲ 307,494
		Variable Customers	18,281	28,893
		Semi-Fixed Customers	0	54,888
		Fixed Customers	289,534	554,287
	Variable Customers		228,106	142,191
		Variable Customers	▲ 62,677	▲ 22,472
		Semi-Fixed Customers	218,400	164,663
		Fixed Customers	72,384	0
	Semi-Fixed Customers		1,009,000	342,596
		Variable Customers	70,511	23,542
		Semi-Fixed Customers	▲ 436,799	▲ 235,233
		Fixed Customers	1,375,288	554,287
	Fixed Customers		▲ 384,212	▲ 491,558
		Variable Customers	2,612	0
		Semi-Fixed Customers	47,478	62,729
		Fixed Customers	▲ 434,301	▲ 554,287

in Table 1, column 1 was developed into variance from expected change rate and variance from discrepancy with expected change rate as shown in Table 2.[4,5]

---

[4]Refer to Matsuoka and Suzuki (2009) for the method to calculate each variance.

[5]To protect the company's confidentiality, the number of customers is kept secret. Also, please note that the results of the variance analysis were modified from the actual numbers.

Table 2. Development into variance from expected change rate and variance from discrepancy with expected change rate.

(Unit: $10)	t period		Variance from expected change rate	Variance from discrepancy with expected change rate
Acquisition Variance	285,530	→	421,729	▲ 136,199
Defection Variance	▲ 281,778	→	▲ 380,992	99,215
New Customers	▲ 109,819	→	▲ 208,656	98,837
Variable Customers	▲ 32,103	→	▲ 32,379	276
Semi-Fixed Customers	▲ 70,570	→	▲ 41,943	▲ 28,627
Fixed Customers	▲ 69,286	→	▲ 98,014	28,728
Transition Variance	323,803	→	1,160,021	▲ 825,478
New Customers	330,574	→	779,291	▲ 442,954
New Customers	▲ 307,494	→	▲ 307,494	0
Variable Customers	28,893	→	28,601	288
Semi-Fixed Customers	54,888	→	0	54,183
Fixed Customers	554,287	→	1,058,184	▲ 497,425
Variable Customers	142,191	→	199,635	▲ 56,705
Variable Customers	▲ 22,472	→	▲ 22,894	417
Semi-Fixed Customers	164,663	→	160,765	3,848
Fixed Customers	0	→	61,763	▲ 60,970
Semi-Fixed Customers	342,596	→	716,097	▲ 368,704
Variable Customers	23,542	→	21,013	2,497
Semi-Fixed Customers	▲ 235,233	→	▲ 262,321	26,740
Fixed Customers	554,287	→	957,405	▲ 397,940
Fixed Customers	▲ 491,558	→	▲ 535,001	42,885
Variable Customers	0	→	1,525	▲ 1,505
Semi-Fixed Customers	62,729	→	55,868	6,773
Fixed Customers	▲ 554,287	→	▲ 592,394	37,618

From the results, the president of Company A saw the variance from discrepancy with the expected change rate as a clear demonstration of the momentum of customer relationship building, and evaluated it as "extremely helpful information from the perspective of managers," because "in order for a company to adapt to environmental changes and continue its business, it needs to make changes on its own and create new businesses. For that, simply earning profits from the current business is not enough; it requires an effort to boost the momentum of earning profit and increase the potential growth. The information on whether the momentum of customer relationship building is increasing, which is provided by the BMVA, helps evaluate that kind of effort."

In fact, as the president of Company A addressed his employees about the importance of not only the fixed customers but also of acquiring new ones — using the BMVA — his intention of "staying aware of the acquisition of new customers while maintaining the relationship with fixed customers" started to permeate through the sales department employees. In addition, considering that retaining fixed customers and acquiring new ones relied on having attractive products, Company A launched a product development department and started developing its own products: "(Grasping the customers' dynamics with the Bathtub Model) motivated us to develop our products and created a virtuous cycle," the president said.

Looking back at the changes in management accounting and operations due to the series of management reforms, the president of Company A says, "the awareness of fixed and new customers (before and after the introduction of FRA) is different. After turning our fixed operating profit positive in 2009[6] and overcoming difficulties related to the Great East Japan Earthquake, we have succeeded in securing fixed operating profit for consecutive periods." He also determined that FRA and the BMVA provided Company A with greater financial stability and growth.

4.6 *Barriers to change*

FRA remained operational after its introduction. However, this does not mean the entire reform went smoothly; it faced resistance from management and sales departments.

As previously mentioned, the president reformed employees' awareness while implementing the structural changes in the company, despite

---

[6]According to the president of Company A, the market was in dire conditions following the Lehman Brothers' collapse.

opposing forces. As part of this process, he also made changes to the management accounting system under the guidance of the creator of FRA. The president states that, while some of the employees supported him and collaborated with the reform, the opposing forces eventually left Company A.

This suggests that when a barrier to management accounting change arises, leadership from the president and senior managers, and momentum for change, are required to break through it.

5. Discussion

This section discusses the results of the case study of the introduction of FRA to Company A. The case suggests the following two main points.

First, for a company to introduce FRA, in addition to the facilitators, motivators, and catalysts discussed by Innes and Mitchell (1990), leadership and momentum for change to overcome barriers, as discussed by Cobb *et al.* (1995), are indispensable. In Company A, though a motivator (deterioration of business environment), catalysts (decrease in operating profit rate, implementation of management reform, encounter with FRA), and facilitators (support from IT and accounting staff) existed, those were only necessary conditions; barrier to change (resistance from management and sales departments) posed a risk to the changes in management accounting. Hence, to continue the management reform and benefit from the momentum for change — direct guidance in introducing FRA by its creator and the BMVA by the authors — the president of Company A himself took the leadership and broke through the barriers to change. This is how the introduction and operation of FRA were promoted.

Second, with the introduction of FRA and the BMVA, the awareness that fixed customers are important increased immensely, even among the employees, as did the awareness of acquiring new customers. This then promoted reform in Company A, which started to develop its own products to retain existing fixed customers and acquire new ones. This change in Company A is likely to have reached the first order to second order of change discussed by Laughlin (1991).[7] In other words, a significant shift

---

[7]According to Laughlin (1991), change can be divided into two stages (orders). A first-order change is a minor, temporary shift in structure, process, and systems. A second-order change is a level at which significant changes are accepted by a small group or the entire

would occur across the entire organization, changing not only the management accounting system, but also the beliefs, values, and standards, that is, the so-called DNA of the company.

6. Conclusion

This study applied a case study to demonstrate when companies can introduce FRA from the perspective of management accounting change in a B2B company. More specifically, it demonstrated that in order to introduce FRA, facilitators, motivators, and catalysts alone are not sufficient, as it also requires leadership to overcome barriers and create momentum for change.

For companies considering introducing FRA, identifying the factors that promote or hinder the process represents useful knowledge. Therefore, we believe this paper has practical significance. Additionally, while most previous studies related to FRA, present cases of FRA introduction, and variance analysis along with their results, this study also explains the factors that promote and hinder the introduction of FRA based on theories that rely on previous studies, which gives it theoretical significance.

We conclude this paper with research topics for the future. Since this study is a case study in a single company, it does not necessarily explain completely the factors that cause changes in management accounting systems or its promoting and hindering factors. Therefore, additional studies on companies that introduced FRA will be necessary. We will also need to conduct surveys to generalize the hypotheses derived.

References

Anthony, R. N. and Govindarajan, V. 2007. *Management Control Systems,* 12th, McGraw-Hill/Irwin, New York, NY.

Burns, J. and Vaivio, J. 2001. Management Accounting Change, *Management Accounting Research*, 12(4), 389–402.

---

organization. The second order represents the level at which not only the system, but the company's beliefs, values, and standards, that is, its DNA, changes.

Cobb, I., Helliar, C., and Innes, J. 1995. Management Accounting Change in a Bank, *Management Accounting Research*, 6(2), 155–175.

Innes, J. and Mitchell, F. 1990. The Process of Change in Management Accounting: Some Field Study Evidence, *Management Accounting Research*, 1(1), 3–19.

Kasurinen, T. 2002. Exploring Management Accounting Change: The Case of Balanced Scorecard Implementation, *Management Accounting Research*, 13(3), 323–343.

Laughlin, R. C. 1991. Environmental Disturbances and Organizational Transitions and Transformations: Some Alternative Models, *Organization Studies*, 12(2), 209–232.

Libby, T. and Waterhouse, J. H. 1996. Predicting Change in Management Accounting Systems, *Journal of Management Accounting Research*, 8, 137–150.

Matsuoka, K. and Suzuki, K. 2008. A Variance Analysis in Fixed Revenue Accounting: The Framework and a Case Study for Customer Relationship Variance Analysis, *The Journal of Cost Accounting Research*, 32(1), 85–97 (In Japanese).

Matsuoka, K. and Suzuki, K. 2009. Variance Deployment based on the Bathtub Model Framework in Fixed Revenue Accounting, *The Journal of Cost Accounting Research*, 33(2), 45–58 (In Japanese).

Scapens, R. W., Turley, S., and Burns, J. 1996. *External Reporting and Management Decisions*, CIMA, London.

Suzuki, K. 2007. A Consideration on the Applicability of Fixed Revenue Accounting, *The Accounting*, 171(2), 46–57 (In Japanese).

Suzuki, K. 2012. Fixed Revenue Accounting, In Saki, A. and Suzuki, K. A Study for Developing the New Models of Strategic Management Control, *Memoirs of Institute of Social Sciences, Meiji University*, 50(2), 24–80 (In Japanese).

Williams, J. J. and Seaman, A. E. 2001. Predicting Change in Management Accounting Systems: National Culture and Industry Effects, *Accounting, Organizations and Society*, 26(4–5), 443–460.

Yin, R. K. 2014. *Case Study Research: Design and Methods,* 5th Edition, SAGE Publications, California, CA.

Yoshida, E. 2003. A Meaning of Management Accounting Change Research, *The Journal of Business Studies Ryukoku University*, 43(2), 100–112 (In Japanese).

Part 4

Related Topics
in Management Accounting

Chapter 8

Goal Congruence between Top Management and Divisional Managers

Kazuyoshi Morimoto

1. Introduction

This study investigates how congruence can be achieved between a firm's top management goal and its divisional managers' performance goals. Goal congruence exists when divisional managers spontaneously take actions to achieve organizational goals assigned by top management over personal interests. In this study, the author uses the theory of agency relationships to analyze such goal congruence.[1] The top management, who makes decisions to maximize the value of the firm to shareholders, acts as the principal. Further, the top management controls divisional managers who act as agents that try their best in pursuing the organizational goal of decentralized units. However, the divisional managers may prefer leisure to hard work and not always act in the best interests of the top management. The author therefore proposes a measure of performance of divisional managers and an incentive scheme to motivate them, to realize goal congruence.

The chapter is organized as follows. Section 2 analyzes congruence between top management's goal and divisional managers' performance

---

[1]This study examines agency relationships between top management and divisional managers in light of the LEN agency model (Spremann, 1987, pp. 3–37). The set of assumptions in the LEN agency model is as follows: (1) wage paid to agent is a linear function of performance measure; (2) utility function of agent is exponential; (3) risk is normally distributed.

goals in the case of management based on shareholders' value. In Section 3, following a setting proposed by Dutta and Reichelstein (2002) and Wagenhofer (2003), the author divides the divisional managers' activities into two categories: investment and management. Further, following the work of Rogerson (1997), who analyzed the agency relationship between owners of the firm and managers, it is clear that top management can induce divisional managers to make the optimal investment decision by evaluating the divisional managers' performance on the basis of residual income. Section 4 discusses the consistency between the performance measure of divisional managers and that of workers within each division. The work of Liang *et al.* (2008) has contributed significantly to this study. However, this study has chosen a different assumption from that in their study. Section 5 reconsiders the agency model that places emphasis on providing monetary incentives and explores the principal–agent relationship in the Japanese automobile industry from the viewpoints of sustainability and moral economy. Section 6 presents the conclusion of the study.

2. Management Based on Shareholders' Value

There exists an agency relationship between the shareholders of a firm and the firm's top management. The shareholders act as the principal and engage the top management as the agent to manage the entire organization of a company. However, if monitoring carried out by shareholders is insufficient, the top management will not always make optimal decisions and take actions from the shareholders' viewpoint. Therefore, in such a situation, some divergence of interest will always exist between shareholders and top management. Shareholders will attempt to limit the divergence from their interests by establishing appropriate incentives for top management. For example, many firms use stock options or bonus payments based on measured performance to motivate top management. As a result, nowadays, the firm's top management accepts the shareholders' goal as the organizational goal and exerts efforts toward attaining this goal. This recent transition to managing the organization based on shareholders' value is a historical consequence of negotiations and struggles among various influential stakeholders for a long time (Monden, 2016, p. 3).

Now, according to finance theory, the value of a firm can be measured as follows[2] (Wakasugi, 2004, p.149):

The value of a firm = The value of shareholders' equity

+ The value of the firm's debt

As shown in Eq. (1), the value of a firm, which is the sum of both the values mentioned above, is measured using the present value of future free cash flows. Here, $(1 + r)^{-1}$ denotes the discount factor of the principal and r denotes the principal's cost of capital.

$$V_{FCF} = \frac{FCF_1}{(1+r)^1} + \frac{FCF_2}{(1+r)^2} + \ldots + \frac{FCF_\infty}{(1+r)^\infty} = \sum_{t=1}^{\infty} \frac{FCF_t}{(1+r)^t} \tag{1}$$

According to Monden (2001), in addition to the valuation method based on free cash flows (FCF method) in Eq. (1), there is another valuation method based on residual income (RI method). As shown in Eq. (2), the value of a firm measured using the RI method is equal to the book value of invested capital CP_1 plus the present value of the future residual income stream.

$$V_{RI} = CP_1 + \sum_{t=1}^{\infty} \frac{RI_t}{(1+r)^t} \tag{2}$$

The firm's value based on free cash flows V_{FCF} is mathematically equal to the firm's value based on residual income V_{RI}. The equality of both Eqs. (1) and (2) has been mathematically demonstrated by many researchers. Thus, Eq. (3) is obtained as shown below.

$$V_{FCF} = \sum_{t=1}^{\infty} \frac{FCF_t}{(1+r)^t} = CP_1 + \sum_{t=1}^{\infty} \frac{RI_t}{(1+r)^t} = V_{RI} \tag{3}$$

---

[2] The value of shareholders' equity implies the market value of the firm's shares. The market value would be roughly the number of outstanding shares multiplied by current price of a share. Because share prices are formed in marketplaces, the formation of share prices is influenced by various factors, including speculative funds. Thus, the author assumes that the market value of the firm's shares reflects the underlying economic fundamentals of a firm.

The two above-mentioned valuation methods, the FCF method and the RI method, can also be used to measure the business value of each division in multidivisional firms. The business value of each division is measured by the present value of future free cash flows in the same way as Eq. (1). As understood from Eq. (3), if the divisional managers try their best to increase the periodical amount of their residual income, the business value of each division will increase through the productive efforts of the divisional managers.

$$\sum_{t=1}^{\infty} \frac{\text{FCF}_t}{(1+r)^t} - CP_1 = \sum_{t=1}^{\infty} \frac{RI_t}{(1+r)^t} \qquad (4)$$

Now, Eq. (3) can be rewritten as Eq. (4) to explain the principal-agent relationship between top management and divisional managers who are considered as investment centers. If the divisional managers continue to make investment decisions in such a way that the left-hand side of Eq. (4) is positive, the divisional managers' investment decisions enhance shareholders' value as much as the difference between the business value measured by the present value of future free cash flows and the book value of invested capital. The difference is the increment of the free cash flows as well as the total amount of residual income that the divisional managers should acquire on behalf of top management. Thus, when top management evaluates divisional managers on the basis of the residual income performance measure and the divisional managers are paid proportionally to the residual income in each period, goal congruence between top management and divisional managers can be achieved.

3. Investment Activities of Divisional Managers

When each divisional manager is considered as an investment center, top management delegates the authority of investment decisions to the manager because it expects the manager to have superior information regarding the profitability of an investment project. In such a situation, top management, who wants to obtain this superior information from the divisional managers, would induce the managers to make optimal investment decisions that maximize shareholders' value. Following the work of Rogerson (1997), this section thoroughly explores the problem of selecting a measure of performance of a divisional manager to achieve goal congruence.

To begin with, suppose there are $T + 1$ periods such that $t \in \{0, 1, \ldots, T\}$. Top management contracts with divisional managers for managing each division. According to the specified contract, it is assumed that the managers choose a level of investment in period 0 and then exert unobservable managerial effort in each period $1, \ldots, T$. The initial cash investment in period 0 will generate cash flows in future periods, and the level of managerial effort also affects the division's cash flows in each period.

Let b denote the level of initial cash investment chosen by the divisional managers in period 0, that is, b is an investment cost. Further, let x_t denote the cash flows in period t generated from the initial cash investment. Furthermore, let s denote the divisional manager's superior information regarding the profitability of the investment. Thus, the cash flows received in period t owing to the divisional manager's investment decision are denoted by $x_t(b, s)$.

In addition, let m_t denote the level of managerial effort of divisional managers in period t, and let $y_t(m_t)$ denote the cash flows generated in period t owing to their managerial effort in period t. Thus, the cash flows received in period t by the division are determined by Eq. (5). Here, ε_t denotes a random variable that is normally distributed.

$$c_t = x_t(b, s) + y_t(m_t) + \varepsilon_t \qquad (5)$$

$x_t(b, s)$ and $y_t(m_t)$ are additively separable in Eq. (5). This implies that the level of initial cash investment can be determined independently of the managerial effort levels in each period. The additive structure of the total cash flows in Eq. (5) may suggest that the hidden information and the hidden action problem are separable; however, these two problems are actually intertwined (Dutta and Reichelstein, 2002, p. 256).

It is assumed that the investment remains equally productive over its entire lifetime, and the cash flows received by the division from the investment are uniform for every period (Rogerson, 1997, p. 776). Based on this assumption, if the periodical amount of cash flows, which are uniform for every period, are denoted by $\bar{x}$, then $x_t(b, s)$ can be written as $\bar{x}(b, s)$. Eq. (5) accordingly reduces to Eq. (6).

$$c_t = \overline{x}(b, s) + y_t(m_t) + \varepsilon_t \tag{6}$$

On the other hand, assume that top management is risk-neutral and their cost of capital is denoted by r^* $\{r^*/0 \leq r^* < \infty\}$. The investment level that maximizes the expected discounted cash flows for top management is the level of maximizing Eq. (7), which denotes the net present value (NPV) of an investment project.

$$\sum_{t=1}^{T} \frac{\overline{x}(b, s) + y_t(m_t)}{(1+r^*)^t} - b \tag{7}$$

When $\sum_{t=1}^{T} (1+r^*)^{-t}$ is alternatively expressed in terms of $\rho(r^*)$, Eq. (7) can be rewritten as Eq. (8) as follows:

$$\rho(r^*)\overline{x}(b,s) + \rho(r^*)y_t(m_t) - b \tag{8}$$

Let us differentiate Eq. (8) with respect to b and set the resulting derivative equal to zero. The result is $\rho(r^*)\bar{x}_b(b, s) - 1 = 0$. Solving the resulting equation for discounted cash flow maximization, we obtain Eq. (9).

$$\overline{x}_b(b, s) = \frac{1}{\rho(r^*)} \tag{9}$$

Now, suppose that the wage payments for divisional managers are based on accounting income levels. In this case, an allocation rule dividing the investment cost to each period influences the divisional managers' wages. Let a_t denote the investment cost allocated to period t from the total investment cost. Thus, a_t is the allocation rate. If b dollars are invested, then a cost of $a_t \cdot b$ dollars is allocated to period t. A cost of $a_t \cdot b$ dollars represents the periodical cost charges imposed on the divisional manager.

Furthermore, suppose that the accounting income in period t is defined by $c_t - a_t \cdot b$. In this case, by substituting Eq. (6) into $c_t - a_t \cdot b$, the accounting income in period t is given by Eq. (10).

$$\pi_t = \overline{x}(b, s) + y_t(m_t) - a_t \cdot b + \varepsilon_t \tag{10}$$

Let us differentiate Eq. (10) with respect to b. Setting the resulting derivative equal to zero and solving the resulting equation for accounting income maximization, we obtain Eq. (11).

$$\bar{x}_b(b, s) = a_t \tag{11}$$

As a result, we can recognize from Eqs. (9) and (11) that the allocation rule induces the divisional manager to make the optimal investment decision conditional on $a_t = 1/\rho(r^*)$.

Rogerson describes a property of the allocation rule in that the discounted values of the allocated shares sum to one (Rogerson, 1997, p. 779). This property of the allocation rule can be showed in Eq. (12).

$$\sum_{t=1}^{T} \frac{a_t}{(1+r^*)^t} = a_t \sum_{t=1}^{T} \frac{1}{(1+r^*)^t} = 1 \tag{12}$$

By substituting $\sum_{t=1}^{T}(1+r^*)^{-t} = \rho(r^*)$ in Eq. (12), we obtain $a_t \cdot \rho(r^*) = 1$. Finally, Eq. (13) is obtained.

$$a_t = \frac{1}{\rho(r^*)} \tag{13}$$

A unique allocation rule that satisfies Eq. (13) is called the annuity allocation rule. According to Rogerson (1997), only the annuity allocation rule induces managers to choose the optimal investment level; the income measure created by this annuity allocation rule is usually referred to as residual income. In addition, Reichelstein (1997) describes that there is indeed no performance measure other than residual income for which the present value of the cost charges imposed on the manager, that is, depreciation plus interest on the book value, is equal to the value of the investment (Reichelstein, 1997, p. 158). As a consequence, top management can induce divisional managers to choose the optimal investment level when concluding an income-based wage contract with the managers and relying on performance measures based on residual income for providing incentives to the managers.

4. Managerial Activities of Divisional Managers

If top management evaluates the divisional manager's performance on the basis of residual income, as previously mentioned, the top management can induce the managers to make the optimal investment decisions. Thus, top management should offer a linear contract to divisional managers consisting of a fixed wage and an incentive wage on the residual income measure, that is, $w = F + k \cdot \pi^{RI}$. Here, w denotes the total amount of wages, F denotes the fixed wage, $k \cdot \pi^{RI}$ denotes the incentive wage based on residual income, and k denotes the bonus coefficient.

However, the divisional managers not only serve the role of making investment decisions but also take managerial actions for achieving the organizational goal. Further, they serve the role of eliciting members' services to the cooperative system, while satisfying the personal motives of organizational members. According to Barnard's theory of cooperative behavior in formal organizations, organizations can exist only when the contributions of the members' personal efforts, which constitute the ener-gies of the organization, are consistent with the supply of incentives that satisfy the motives of the members within the organization (Barnard, 1938, pp. 139–160). In this section, the author discusses the consistency between the performance measure of divisional managers and the perfor-mance measure of workers within each division.

According to Liang et al. (2008), it is assumed that top management contracts with n workers who exert unobservable efforts. Let $N = \{1, 2,..., n\}$ denote the set of workers and e_i denote each effort choice of n workers ($i \in N$). Liang et al. (2008) consider a manager who conducts monitoring activities for n workers in their model. Each worker actively cooperates with the team and produces joint output under the manager's supervision. It is also assumed that the manager exerts monitoring effort m, which reduces the variance of the team performance measure. According to Liang et al. (2008), the team performance measure h is given by Eq. (14).

$$h = \sum_{i \in N} e_i + \varepsilon, \quad \text{where } \varepsilon \sim N\left(0, \frac{G(n)\sigma^2}{m}\right) \qquad (14)$$

Here, ε denotes the noise term, which is normally distributed with mean zero and variance $G(n)\sigma^2/m$. σ measures the uncertainty in performance measurement. $G(n)$ denotes the noise in performance measurement that increases with the number of workers, n. The noise becomes larger as the team size grows because of problems with coordination or communication difficulties.

Liang *et al.* (2008) consider that the manager's effort m reduces the variance of the team performance measure h, while the workers' effort increases its mean. Because the efforts exerted by all workers and the manager are unobservable, the top management offers a linear contract to them to motivate the supply of their efforts. In the model of Liang *et al.* (2008), thus, each worker receives wage $w_i = F_i + k_i \cdot h$ and the manager receives wage $w = F + k \cdot h$. In their model, the managers' efforts do not affect the expectation of their wages; however, their effort decreases the variance of the team performance measure. The study chooses to emphasize the monitoring role of managers, leaving other managerial functions, such as fulfilling direct productive tasks, as second-order effects (Liang *et al.*, 2008, p. 797).

This study shows that top management offers a linear contract $w = F + k \cdot \pi^{RI}$ to divisional managers. In this study, it is assumed that the productive efforts of the divisional managers affect the expectation of their wages. Therefore, the divisional managers increase the division's residual income in each period to receive a higher wage. Based on this assumption, however, the performance measure of divisional managers and that of workers under their control must be consistent. This implies that consistency between π^{RI} and h must be secured to achieve goal congruence between the divisional manager and the workers within each division. This study considers that it is important to establish a management control system for securing consistency between π^{RI} and h. Some management control systems in Japanese firms tie the residual income measure as an organizational goal to the performance measures of workers. An example of such systems is the key performance index (KPI) system based on policy development of Japanese total quality management (TQM).

The KPI system breaks the residual income measure of divisional managers into individual KPIs for various workers throughout the layers of the organization, based on policy development of Japanese TQM, as a tool for implementing top management's policy (Monden, 2001, pp. 342–347). In the KPI system, the target amount of residual income is first broken down into functional operating processes, and value drivers that influence major cost, revenue, and asset items of each functional operating process are then identified. Some examples of value drivers are reduction of manufacturing costs, just-in-time (JIT) production, quality improvement, and reduction of distribution inventory. Value drivers are further broken down into individual KPIs for various workers within each division.

The lean production system uses various non-financial measures such as KPIs at the manufacturing floor level. For example, there are non-financial measures such as reduction rate of manufacturing costs, production lead time, appearance rate of defective units, and inventory turnover period. Recently, according to Wang and Monden (2016), there have been many proposals for integrating such non-financial measures into accounting measures to understand the overall effects of the lean production system on company wide performance (Wang and Monden, 2016, p. 147). Wang and Monden (2016), using residual income as an accounting measure, define JIT residual income as follows:

$$\text{JIT residual income} = \text{contribution margin} - \text{plant workforce expenses}$$

$$- \text{cost of capital} \times \text{closing inventory}$$

The lean production system divides an organization into a lot of small teams on the manufacturing floor, and the JIT residual income measure is used as a measure of performance of team leaders. Needless to say, the JIT residual income measure connects with KPIs at the manufacturing floor level. Moreover, because the residual income of each division is an aggregate of every JIT residual income within each division, there is consistency between the divisional residual income measure and the JIT residual income measure. JIT residual income is a basis to evaluate shareholders' value. Therefore, team leaders can contribute to the enhancement of shareholder value while trying their best at increasing JIT residual income (Wang and Monden, 2016, p. 153).

In addition, the target amount of residual income should be the remainder after compensating for the minimum rate of return required by shareholders and top management. There is usually a gap between the target amount of residual income expected by top management and the actual residual income gained by divisional managers. To fill this gap, they completely try to improve the actual KPI of each worker by offering pecuniary rewards such as bonuses and non-pecuniary rewards such as promotions or demotions.

5. Viewpoints of Sustainability and Moral Economy

The above analysis focuses on the principal–agent relationship between top management, who is required to enhance shareholder value, and divisional managers, who are considered as an investment center in multidivisional firms. As noted above, the value of a firm to its shareholders increases when the divisional managers try their best to increase the periodical amount of their residual income. Accordingly, if top management uses the residual income as the divisional managers' performance measure to control their performance, the top management can fulfill their fiduciary responsibility to shareholders. Moreover, if the top management pays divisional managers monetary compensation proportional to residual income, goal congruence between top management and divisional managers can be achieved.

However, today's society expects organizations to grow sustainably. Therefore, if the firm's top management agree to these expectations of sustainability, that is, the simultaneous pursuit of profit, people, and planet, the top management must devise an incentive scheme to motivate divisional managers and other employees by considering not only economic incentives but also social motivations encouraging moral behavior and environmental protection. Because traditional economics and corporate finance considered merely economic profit to explain the behavior of firms, they have some limitations in terms of sustainability. Thus, we need to consider the behavioral (human) aspect of the firm (Monden, 2017, p. 87).

Bowles (2016), the author of the book, "The Moral Economy", insists that fines, rewards, and other material incentives often do not work very well and that incentives cannot alone build the foundations of good governance. According to Bowles (2016), the greater use of monetary incentives to guide individual behavior promotes self-interest, so that ethical and other-regarding motivations essential to good governance may be undermined by such excessive monetary incentives. In other words, the greater use of monetary incentives may even compromise the social norms essential to the working of markets themselves. Consequently, Bowles (2016) wishes to advance the policy paradigm of synergy between economic incentives and ethical and other-regarding motivations (Bowles, 2016, p. 7).

Although this study investigates the principal–agent relationship between top management and divisional managers while placing emphasis on the supply of monetary incentives, it examines the principal–agent relationship in the Japanese automobile industry from the viewpoints of sustainability and moral economy emphasized by Bowles (2016). In this agency relationship, the automaker acts as the principal and the parts manufacturers act on behalf of the automaker as agents.

As has been widely discussed, automakers in Japan have maintained longstanding transactional relations with parts manufacturers and established collaborative and reciprocal relations in the form of *keiretsu* alignments. According to the study by Asanuma and Kikutani (1992), the core automaker absorbs the risks borne by parts manufacturers in the contractual practices regarding parts transactions. Asanuma (1985) also describes the absorption of risks as follows. The automaker bears the risk of tooling and die costs and other specific capital investments and guarantees a certain volume of production to parts manufacturers. Moreover, the automaker goes beyond risk sharing and directly bears costs for the purchase of tooling and die on behalf of parts manufacturers (Asanuma, 1985, p. 51). On the other hand, the automaker accepts a rise in the price of the parts when there is an increase in raw material prices; however, energy costs are handled differently. The automaker resists including energy price changes as a variable part of the price of parts. During the first oil crisis of 1973, however, automakers agreed to a rise in the price of parts by including energy price changes as an exception to the rule (Asanuma, 1985, p. 43).

On the other hand, according to Monden (2017), the automaker collaborates with the parts manufacturers for reducing the cost of parts in the product development stage as well as the mass production stage. Moreover, the joint margin created from the reduced costs is impartially shared between the automaker and the parts manufacturers based on their ratio of contribution to the cost reduction. If 40% of the reduced costs were due to using the automaker's ideas, then 40% of the joint margin created from reducing the cost of parts will be allocated as a reduction in the price of parts to the automaker, and 60% of the joint margin will be allocated as an increase in profit to the parts manufacturers. Such collaborative innovations and improvements for reducing the cost of parts can not only create a win–win relationship through the fair allocation of joint margins, but also provide incentives to enhance the morale of employees of both the automaker and the parts manufacturers and contribute to the development and production of attractive products for end customers (Monden, 2017, p. 89).

As previously mentioned, regarding the principal–agent relationship in the Japanese automobile industry, the automaker establishes collaborative and reciprocal relations with the parts manufacturers. The automaker absorbs the risks, which the parts manufacturers ought to bear, and collaborates with the parts manufacturers for creating joint margins. Moreover, the joint margin is fairly allocated between both the parties. When judging from such contractual practices, we cannot explain the cooperative behaviors of both the automaker and the parts manufacturers merely from their self-interest motivations. Thus, we need to give their cooperative behaviors a theoretical explanation while considering their other-regarding and reciprocal motivations.

6. Conclusions

The purpose of this study is to design a performance measure for divisional managers and devise an incentive scheme to motivate the managers. By judging from the mathematical equality of both the FCF method and the RI method, the study first identified that the shareholders' value increased when divisional managers gained the periodical amount of their residual income. Then, it was found that top management could induce divisional managers to make investment decisions for enhancing shareholder value when evaluating the managers' performance on the basis of residual income. Further, it was found that goal congruence between top management and divisional managers could be achieved when the managers were rewarded proportionally to the residual income to motivate them. In conclusion, the system of selecting residual income as a divisional manager's performance measure and devising an incentive scheme based on this measure is most suitable in firms using management based on shareholders' value.

Furthermore, from the example of Japanese management control systems that connect the residual income measure to the performance measure of workers, it can be concluded that it is essential to establish a management control system for securing consistency between the performance measures of divisional managers and those of workers within each division.

Finally, the agency models that place emphasis on providing economic and monetary incentives were reconsidered. Here, the study explores the agency relationship in the Japanese automobile industry from the viewpoints of sustainability and moral economy. Further, the study confirmed the need to consider not only self-interest motivations but also other-regarding and reciprocal motivations to explain the principal–agent relationship in the Japanese automobile industry. Thus, the author would like to emphasize the need to devise an incentive scheme considering the synergy between monetary incentives and other-regarding motivations for attaining sustainability in the modern community.

References

Asanuma, B. 1985. The Organization of Parts Purchases in the Japanese Automotive Industry, *Japanese Economic Studies,* 32–53.

Asanuma, B. and Kikutani, T. 1992. Risk Absorption in Japanese Subcontracting: A Microeconometric Study of the Automobile Industry, *Journal of the Japanese and International Economies,* 6(1), 1–29.

Barnard, C. I. 1938. *The Functions of the Executive,* Harvard University Press, Cambridge and London.

Bowles, S. 2016. *The Moral Economy: Why Good Incentives Are No Substitute for Good Citizens,* Yale University Press, New Haven and London.

Dutta, S. and Reichelstein, S. 2002. Controlling Investment Decisions: Depreciation- and Capital Charges, *Review of Accounting Studies,* 7, 253–281.

Liang, P. J., Rajan, M.V., and Ray, K. 2008. Optimal Team Size and Monitoring in Organizations, *The Accounting Review,* 83(3), 789–822.

Monden,Y. 2001. *Managerial Accounting,* Tokyo, Zeimukeiri Kyokai (In Japanese).

Monden,Y. 2016. *Seminar in Managerial Accounting,* Tokyo, Zeimukeiri Kyokai (In Japanese).

Monden,Y. 2017. Solving the Wage Differentials Throughout the Supply Chain by Collaborative Innovations for Changing the Parts Prices and Costs. In Hamada, K. and Hiraoka, S. (Eds.), *Japanese Management and International Studies,* Vol.13, World Scientific Publishing Ltd., Singapore, pp. 67–93.

Reichelstein, S. 1997. Investment Decisions and Managerial Performance Evaluation, *Review of Accounting Studies,* 2, 157–180.

Rogerson, W. 1997. Intertemporal Cost Allocation and Managerial Investment Incentives: A Theory Explaining the Use of Economic Value Added as a Performance Measure, *Journal of Political Economy,* 105(4), 770–795.

Spremann, K. 1987. Agent and Principal. In Bamberg, G. and Spremann, K. (Eds.), *Agency Theory, Information, and Incentives,* Springer Verlag, Berlin and Heidelberg, pp. 3–37.

Wagenhofer, A. 2003. Accrual-Based Compensation, Depreciation and Investment Decisions, *European Accounting Review,* 12(2), 287–309.

Wakasugi, T. 2004. *Corporate Finance,* Tokyo, Chuokeizai-Sha (In Japanese).

Wang, Z. and Monden, Y. 2016. Financial Performance Measures for the Lean Production System. In Monden, Y. and Minagawa, Y. (Eds.), *Japanese Management and International Studies,* Vol. 12, World Scientific Publishing Ltd., Singapore, pp. 147–159.

Chapter 9

Budgeting and Vertical/Horizontal Interaction in New Product Development — A Case Study in Car Navigation System Development

Masanobu Nakamura

1. Introduction

1.1 *Background*

In product development by an enterprise, it has been pointed out that a product development project organized across functional departments has a big influence on the competitiveness of the enterprise. By utilizing cross functional projects, it is expected to use the resources of the enterprise strategically and combine technology and resources effectively with coordination between projects (Nobeoka, 1996).

In research of the management control system (MCS) on product development, it has been pointed out frequently that it is important for MCS to promote horizontal interaction between functional departments involved. What is expected is that it contributes to developing products with high customer appeal while allowing many people to demonstrate creative ingenuity regardless of department at the same time and with efficiency (Monden, 1994).

In recent years, in addition to the above points, it is necessary to consider the heightening of strategic uncertainty. Simons (1995, p. 94), defined strategic uncertainties as "the uncertainties and contingencies that could threaten or invalidate the current strategy of the business". He proposed interactive control as a means of managing these uncertainties. In this concept, it is pointed out that it is necessary for the superiors to encourage the subordinates to promote strategy implementation and simultaneously provide information on strategic uncertainty and tackle change and emergence of strategy. Simons (2005) suggests moving beyond vertical interaction between superiors and subordinates to handle strategic uncertainties and move to an interactive network with horizontal interaction between functional departments as well as vertical interaction.

1.2 *The purpose of this research*

The purpose of this research is to clarify how the budget for development cost is managed within the development organization and vertical/horizontal interaction is promoted on the premise of product development by the project teams organized across functional departments.

Project & Program budgeting (Pbudgeting), proposed by Suzuki and Matsuoka (2004) as a budget management framework based on project, positions program as a business plan set for strategy execution and project as activity for executing program. It allocates organization resources to program, organizes and executes the budget based on a project basis, repeats performance evaluation in the middle, and assumes there is a correction of budget and resource allocation for project and program and the strategy modification. The value being aimed at with program is set to be equal to or more than the sum of the values of project. Regarding its effectiveness, Nakamura *et al.* (2012) confirmed the effect of reducing the development cost by flexibly correcting the budget within project and among projects. However, details on how vertical and horizontal information sharing and adjustment are promoted among stakeholders is unknown.

1.3 *Research method*

Participant observation was conducted to clarify through budgeting how budget and actual information were shared including other development-related information and whether coordination was being carried out between superiors and subordinate managers and also responsible people/ members of project. In product development, projects budget adjustment is made according to the change of specifications of the target function, work schedule, membership, etc. However, actual observation lead to clarification of the factors that promote interaction.

The research site of this research is the development-related department of the car navigation business division of car parts manufacturer. Product development project was carried out within the department by customer. Programs were set up by bundling projects, and it was focused on information sharing and adjustment among stakeholders through the kind of budgeting. In the participant observation, there were no business roles, and participants were permitted to attend weekly meetings (within the project team) and monthly meetings by head of department by customer, etc. The observation period was from January 2010 to December 2010.

1.4 *Structure of this research*

The remainder of this chapter is structured as follows: in the next section the literature is reviewed and particular research questions are clarified; the third section introduces a case study on budgeting for new product development cost in the research site A; the fourth section provides case findings. The final section presents some conclusions and future research themes.

2. Literature Review

2.1 *Promotion of vertical interaction*

On the promotion of vertical interaction, research on promoting information sharing and coordination through budget formulation based on participant budget and performance evaluation/budget correction has been studied.

Kishida (2009, 2010) points out that as a way of using budgeting to functionalize interactive control to work encourages information-sharing between subordinates and superiors in budget participation. This point is examined by Otsuka (1998) as an information gathering function. This function is for the superiors to grasp the market trends so that the subordinates and departments in charge understand the problems they face. It is necessary for the superiors to communicate the business policy and the position of the department to subordinates to increase clarity of duties. As a result, it is pointed out that subordinates understand their roles and goals (Parker and Kyj, 2006; Kishida, 2009, 2010), and the effect of clarifying the contents that are to be reported to the superiors has been pointed out (Chenhall and Brownell, 1988; Kishida, 2009).

Based upon the above arguments, first the following is set as RQ1.

RQ1: What kind of budgeting motivates vertical information sharing and coordination between upper managers, subordinate managers, and program/project managers?

2.2 *Promotion of horizontal interaction*

In Japan, interaction in product development has been focused mainly on horizontal interaction between functional departments. Target costing research has pointed out the importance of horizontal interaction and has assumed that Target costing is a mechanism for promoting interaction (Tani, 1994; Horii and Akroyd, 2009; Morofuji, 2009), and organizational structure and organizational culture have been being considered as promoting factors (Kato, 1993; Tani, 1994). In recent years, management of conflict between goals and between departments within an organization has been researched (Yoshida, 2011, 2012).

Other than Target costing research, it has been pointed out that coordination between functional departments is important. For example, Zirger and Maidique (1990) point out the importance of cooperation and coordination between functional departments such as research and development, marketing, manufacturing, etc.

Clark and Fujimoto (1991) assume that a heavyweight product manager should be responsible for creating product concepts, communication, and coordination across functional departments and should make direct contact with the relevant members.

Based upon the above arguments, the following is set as RQ2.

RQ2: How are information sharing and coordination among product development project managers and other project members as a project team promoted through budget management?

2.3 *Mutual relationship of vertical and horizontal interaction*

The idea of a Interactive Network by Simons (2005) is helpful for considering mutual relationships of vertical interaction between the superior and subordinate managers and the horizontal interaction between the functional departments.

Simons (2005) defines an Interactive Network as a structure and a system in which individuals gather information and influence others' decision-making. It is pointed out that it is necessary to turn attention to activities of other departments and other positions in order to create Interactive Network, and it is proposed to set the scope of accountability beyond the scope of control, to set high targets, and to use interactive control, etc.

Senoh and Yokota (2015), based on Simons (2005), assumes that Interactive Network is an extension of the concept of vertical interactive control (Simons 1995) between the superior and the subordinate.

On that basis, because the uncertainty of environments is increasing it is necessary to effectively increase the creativity of the organization and the commitment of its members to it. Vertical interactive control is positioned as a lever to enhance the organization's creativity, and sharing responsibility in cross-functional relationships is positioned as a lever to enhance organizational commitment.

To point out that projects are carried out under program, as Nakamura *et al.* (2012) point out that the project consolidation progresses within program, it is necessary to pay close attention to mutual relationships concerning vertical information sharing and coordination between program and project managers and horizontal information sharing and coordination among project managers.

Based upon the above arguments, the following is set as RQ3.

RQ3: How do vertical and horizontal interactions relate to each other and influence each other through budgeting?

3. The Case Study

3.1 Reason for selection as a research site — A development organization structure in company A

The research site was the car navigation business division of car parts manufacturer A and consolidated annual sales of Company A at the time of research were approximately 3 trillion JPY (see Fig. 1).

As a business division strategy, the strengthening capability of customer car manufacturers to deal with both short-term and medium- to long-term goals was launched, and the development work has been carried out in three departments in total, two customer-specific development departments and the preceding development department. Within the department by customer, product development programs that bundle and manage individual product development projects were set up and individual product development was promoted within that. Program was set with model classification and product composition classification as a unit such as "High grade class of 2011 model". In this case, high grade means product composition classification, and 2011 model means model classification. Under program, project was set as a destination unit like "domestic selling item" and "North American selling item".[1]

Each project team was organized mainly by three people, a project manager from the system development section, a supervising manager from the software development section, and a supervising manager from the hardware development section. The system development section was responsible for promoting orders from the car manufacturer and took responsibility for realizing product specifications. The software development section was responsible for the development of the software making up the product. The hardware development section was responsible for the development of the hardware making up the product. A program manager was appointed to program which bundles project.[2]

---

[1] In the car parts manufacturing company, which was a research site, "model classification" was set according to the model change of the customer's car manufacturer every four years. In addition, the grade of the product was classified into the three grades of luxury goods, standard products, and entry model; "product composition classification" was set according to this, and "destination" was set depending on which region (country) that product was for.
[2] Under the head of department by customer, program manager and chief of section were same level in position. Project members same as project manager belonged to each section, and they participated in project while being registered in each section.

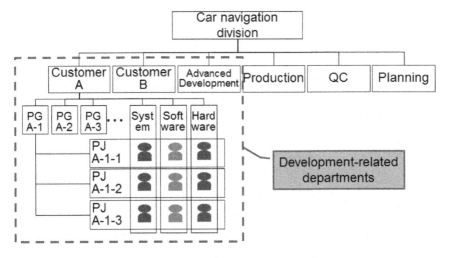

Fig. 1 The organization structure of car navigation business division in research site A.

Project was organized across three sections, such as system development, software development, and hardware development, which were equivalent to functional departments, and according to the development strategy in the business division, department by customer was created. Program under the department by customer and project under program were created. Development cost budget was managed based on project and program. It was judged to be appropriate as a research site due to the organization of development and the development cost management.

3.2 *Product development process in research site A*

Especially, in software development, the development content had a major influence on the increase and decrease of development volume. Therefore, it was important to analyze the difficulty level of development and to analyze whether it is possible to deal with already developed functions at the negotiation stage of product specifications and functions with customers before the start of actual development.

Therefore, in order to prevent unnecessary functional development, contents of development functions and development work volume were appropriately examined mainly by project manager and software and hardware supervising managers with function managers in charge of such aspects as

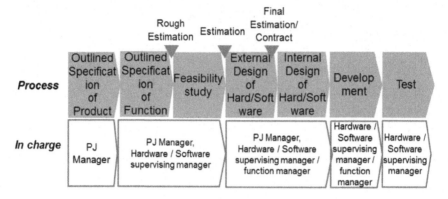

Fig. 2   Product development process in research site A.

navigation function, external link function, audio function, etc. that made up the software.[3] With program manager, commonality of functions between products (between projects) was also considered (see Fig. 2).

Contents that were judged to be very difficult were shared with the advanced development department that undertook basic function development first, separately from product development for customers.[4] After being shared, consideration was also made by customers on whether that department would start work on the realization of the product in the next or later period, or whether it would be realized by product development which had already started.

3.3 Development cost budgeting in research site A

3.3.1 Establishment of development cost budget for individual product development project

For individual product development project, as shown in Fig. 2, the project team calculates the man-hours and development costs until completion from the end of the outline design of hardware and software. With the

---

[3]For example, the navigation function was divided into individual functions such as guidance, route, search, drawing, etc. Function manager was assigned to each function to supervise development work for each individual function which was divided.

[4]Advanced development department had a mission to carry out function development aiming at realization in the future model, not the model which is under development.

customer, the planned delivery price and the planned number of units were confirmed and the contract was agreed. In negotiations with the customer, the planning department calculated the upper limit of development costs and fixed the upper limit of those costs based on the contract content.

The deviation between the calculated amount of the project team and the amount based on the contract was a problem. For that reason, until the contract was agreed, functions and delivered price/number of units were reviewed and negotiations were repeated.

3.3.2 *Budget formulation*

The budget was formulated and managed in a single year.

Prior to the start of the new fiscal year, when the director of the business division created the annual budget plan, the project manager and the hardware, and the software supervising managers/function managers confirmed the next year development plans and estimated annual development costs by checking the upper limit of project development costs. After that, the project manager gathered the estimation and submitted it to the planning department.

The director of the business division, heads of department by customer, the program manager, and chief of each section such as system, hardware, and software confirmed the estimation by project team. Whether each project could comply with the upper limit of development cost was confirmed, readjustment as necessary was carried out with the project manager, and finally the draft by division was confirmed.

The annual budget (which was confirmed after adjustment between the headquarters and the business division) was placed under the control of the project manager and software and hardware supervising managers via program manager (only for half of the year) via head of department by customer. The remaining half was equivalent to the second half, but it was controlled at the discretion of the head of department by customer.

3.3.3 *Budget execution and control*

3.3.3.1 Weekly performance evaluation in project team

Weekly progress meetings were held within the project team after commencement of budget execution.

The project manager, supervising managers of software and hardware, and function managers attended those meetings. First, progress and actual cost were discussed, then the occurrence/solution status of issues, after that the latest work plans were confirmed, the feasibility within the budget was examined, and finally adjustment of content, scheduling, and man-hour planning was carried out.

3.3.3.2 Monthly performance reporting to program manager by project manager

The project manager held weekly meetings in each project team and summarized the following on a monthly basis with software and hardware supervising managers and reported to the program manager.

- Actual versus annual activity plan and budget (variance of budget and actual).
- Planning and implementation of countermeasures for eliminating variance.
- Activity plan and forecast after next month (multiple years).
- Application for additional budget and reasons (as necessary).

The program manager examined the content of the reports for each project, let the project managers examine the adjustment of the development content among projects and the commonality of functions among projects, and then examined the budget adjustment and budget addition.

3.3.3.3 Monthly performance reporting to the head of department by customer by program manager

After the program manager confirmed the results and forecasts of projects under his/her control, a performance evaluation meeting was implemented by the head of each department by customer.

That meeting was jointly conducted in two departments by two heads of department by customer. The program manager, chief of each section (such as system, hardware, and software), and, if necessary, project manager and supervising managers attended.

In this meeting (with the car manufacturer's quadrennial model change in mind), the focus was on whether or not there was a delay in specification or design review, delay in actual development work, or actual versus budget, etc. In particular, the work situation and occurrence of expenses in the domestic and North American sales products (which are be queued by model change) were confirmed. When the actual deviated from the plan and the forecasts were not good, there was a possibility of a bigger risk for product development for other regions, so the details of product specifications and functions, development work, and cost contents were confirmed in detail.

As necessary changes of development content, work plans, and application for additional development cost budget were discussed, the program manager together with the project manager was asked to provide a concrete explanation of the proposed amendments and an additional explanation of circumstances until the escalation of the revision proposal. As a result, planned and budgetary revisions were also approved in many cases. However, it was asked whether it is an escalation after undertaking efforts for each program and project, for example, consultation with car manufacturers concerning development content, work schedule, and development cost. For example, if a request for adding a function from a client came after the contract, if promised promise was made to add that function without adjusting the development cost, it was reprimanded severely.

4. Discussion

Based on the observation of results, an attempt was made to clarify the promoting factors of interaction and each RQ is discussed.

RQ1: What kind of budgeting motivates vertical information sharing and coordination between upper managers, subordinate managers, and program/project managers?

Based on the work plan/budget draft prepared by the project team, the development work by business division was carried out, the performance was evaluated, and the draft for a correction plan was reviewed by the program manager, chief of each section, and head of department by customer directly. Therefore, the sharing of the organization's policy and intentions of the superiors was promoted, and it seemed that the project team was strongly conscious of the success or failure of the project in charge affecting the entire organization. The project team was also committed to the execution of the development work as a business division. For that reason, while aiming at achieving the initial plan (with encouragement by the superiors), it seemed that the project team was proposing a reasonable solution to the problem and a plan for correcting the current plan (which seemed necessary for the product development work) while satisfying the client's request.

The program manager, chief of each section (system, hardware, software), and head of department by customer were constantly required to manage while confirming and correcting the development plan and budget, and they also needed accurate and concrete information on the current situation and prospects. Although, strongly recommended by superiors to achieve the work plan and manage the budget, subordinates were never reprimanded on the deviation between the plan and actual in a blind way and they strongly urged the project team to present solutions and corrective proposals to advance early detection and resolution of issues and create a concrete and realistic review of the corrective plan.

RQ2: How are information sharing and coordination among product development project managers, and other project members as a project team promoted through budget management?

In each project, it is necessary to minimize the amount of development in order to shorten the development period and reduce the development costs. In addition to the specification adjustment (to prevent demand from the car manufacturer from becoming excessive), it was necessary to promote reuse of the existing developed functions and common use of functions among projects. Therefore the project manager (responsible for development of individual products belonging to the system section), the hardware supervising manager (responsible for developing the hardware part of the product belonging to the hardware section), and the software supervising manager (responsible for developing the software part of the product belonging to the software section) have to work as a project team from the initial stage of development (where there was much room for adjustment) and need to consider the product specifications and functions to minimize the amount of development while being conscious of the whole product. It seems to have been motivating to share information and coordinate between functional organizations.

RQ3: How do vertical and horizontal interactions relate to each other and influence each other through budgeting?

In order to shorten the development period and reduce the development costs by restricting the amount of development as an organization, the head of each department by customer (a superior manager), the program manager, and the chief of each section (subordinate managers) instructed the project team to realize specifications and functions strictly with the control of the development amount in mind.

For that reason, the project manager and the software and hardware supervising managers were encouraged to adjust within the team, while trying to restrict the amount of development of individual products and functions. They tried to coordinate with other project teams to promote common use of functions between products and reuse the already developed functions.

Regarding adjustment in each project team and between the project teams, the program manager or chief of sections (who were their superiors) attended the adjustment meetings prompting adjustment and in addition to project, horizontal adjustments between projects, and vertical adjustments between program and project and in each section were promoted.

In addition, the project team was encouraged to make prompt adjustments within project teams and between project teams, as the project team was encouraged to promptly suggest proposals for corrective actions by the head of department by both the customer and the program manager. In addition to weekly meetings within the project team, meetings with other project teams, program managers, and chief of section were held from time to time (see Table 1).

5. Conclusion

On the premise of product development by the project team (organized across functional departments), while shortening the development period and reducing development costs were required, this research tried to clarify how vertical and horizontal interactions were promoted through development cost budgeting within the development related organizations.

Table 1. Factors to promote interaction and the results by RQ.

RQ	Factor to promote interaction	Result
1	• Based on the budget draft prepared by the product development project team, budget formulation and work execution as development department	• Communicating and sharing organizational policies and intentions of superiors • Project team's strong awareness of the impact of project success or failure on the whole organization, its commitment to execute development work as a business unit, and its proposal and examination of problem solving proposals and plan correction proposal
	• Face to face performance evaluation and review of budget revision between project team and superiors	
	• Encouragement to carry out the initial plan and to propose a solution to the problem and a remedy for the plan from the superior to project team	• Presentation from project team to superiors of accurate and concrete information on current situation and prospects • Presentation from project team to superiors of the problem solving plan and plan amendment
2	• Policy thoroughness to minimize development volume as product	
	• Promotion of specification adjustment, reuse of developed functions, and common use of functions among products	• Within the project team, with considering the entire product in mind, examining specifications and functions across the barrier of the functional department
	• From the initial stage of the development process, participation in the development work of all related functional departments	
3	• From the superior to the project team, with the development amount control in mind, strict circumstances and guidance of realization of specifications and functions	• While encouraged to coordinate within the team and to try to control development volumes of individual product and function, promoting coordination with other project teams in order to promote commonality among products and reuse developed functions

(Continued)

Table 1. (*Continued*)

RQ	Factor to promote interaction	Result
	• From superior to project team, promoting coordination within project team and among project teams and superior's presence at coordination meetings	• In addition to hosting weekly meetings within the project team, coordinating meetings between project teams, program managers, department heads, and project teams as appropriate
	• Encouragement for early proposal of plan amendment from superior to project team	

In addition to budgeting within the organization based on the project development cost budget (formulated on the basis of the development cost budget draft created by the project team), as project team was urged to present a correction plan by superiors in addition to achieving budget, vertical and horizontal interactions were promoted in relation to each other by upper and lower managers, project managers, and other members.

However, there are also issues to be researched in the future. In promoting information sharing and coordination, the relevance to personnel evaluation and reward system and the influence of organizational culture have not been confirmed. Regarding product development, research on what kind of MCS including budgeting promotes innovation has been studied, and it is necessary to elucidate this through efforts at the site.

References

Chenhall, R.H. and Brownell, P. 1988. The Effect of Participative Budgeting on Job Satisfaction and Performance: Role Ambiguity as an Intervening Variable, *Accounting, Organizations and Society,* 13(3), 225–233.

Clark, K. B. and Fujimoto. T. 1991. *Product Development Performance: Strategy, Organization, and Management in the World Auto Industry* (Japanese translated version by Tamura, A. was published by Diamond, Tokyo, 2009).

Davila, T. and Wouters, M. 2004. Designing Cost-Competitive Technology Products through Cost Management, *Accounting Horizons,* 18(1), 13–26.

Horii, S. and Akroyd, C. 2009. New Product Development in Buffalo Inc., *Melco Journal of Management Accounting Research,* 2(1), 99–109 (In Japanese).

Kato, Y. 1993. *Production Cost Plan: Strategic Cost Management,* Nihon Keizai Shimbun Inc., Tokyo (In Japanese).

Kishida, T. 2009. Strategic Uncertainty and the Use of Budget Management System, *Journal of the Management Faculty,* 38, 23–53 (In Japanese).

Kishida, T. 2010. An Empirical Analysis on the Use of Budgetary Control and its Effect: The Relationship Mediated by Vertical Information Sharing, *The Journal of Cost Accounting Research,* 34(2), 24–34 (In Japanese).

Monden, Y. 1994. *The Production Cost Plan on which the Price Competitiveness is put and technique of Production Cost Improvement,* Toyo Keizai Inc., Tokyo (In Japanese).

Nakamura, M., Matsuoka, K., and Suzuki, K. 2012. A consideration on the effectiveness of Project & Program Budgeting (Pbudgeting) — Action research in Japanese Pharmaceutical company, *Strategic Management Journal,* 1(2), 137–151 (In Japanese).

Morofuji, Y. 2009. Management Accounting Systems for Cross-Functional Interactions in Target Costing, *Rikkyo Economic Review,* 63(1), 55–67 (In Japanese).

Nobeoka, K. 1996. *Multi Project Strategy: Product Development Management of a Mailbox Lean,* Yuhikaku, Tokyo (In Japanese).

Otsuka, Y. 1998. *Sankagata Yosan Kanri Kenkyuu,* Dobunkan Shuppan, Tokyo (In Japanese).

Parker, R. J. and Kyj, L. 2006. Vertical Information Sharing in the Budgeting Process, *Accounting, Organizations and Society,* 31 (1), 27–45.

Senoh, T. and Yokota, E. 2015. A Preliminary Study on the Effects of Transformational Leadership on Horizontal Interactive Networks, *Melco Journal of Management Accounting Research,* 8(2), 3–16 (In Japanese).

Simons, R. 1995. *Levers of Control: How Managers Use Innovative Control Systems to Drive Strategic Renewal,* Harvard Business School Press, Boston, Massachusetts.

Simons, R. 2005. *Levers of Organization Design: How Managers Use Accountability System for Greater Performance and Commitment,* Harvard Business School Press, Boston, Massachusetts.

Suzuki, K. and Matsuoka, K. 2004. Chapter1 Framework of PBSC. In Ohara, S., Asad, T., and Suzuki, K. (Eds.), *Project Balance Scorecard,* Tokyo: Seisansei Syuppan, 3–32 (In Japanese).

Tani, T. 1994. Interactive Control in the Target Cost Management, *Journal of Economics & Business Administration,* 169(4), 19–38 (In Japanese).

Yoshida, E. 2011. Target Cost Management as Tension Management, *Mita Business Review,* 54(3), 45–59 (In Japanese).

Yoshida, E. 2012. The Role of Management Accounting as Tension Management: An Empirical Analysis of Target Cost Management and Management Control, *Mita Business Review,* 54(6), 75–86 (In Japanese).

Zirger, B. J. and Maidique M. A. 1990. A Model of New Product Development, *Management Science,* 36(7), 867–883.

Chapter 10

Empirical Study of Mechanism of Budgetary Control and *Hoshin Kanri* to Stimulate Autonomous Behavior Based on Theory of *Ba*

Hitomi Toyosaki, Misa Kikyo, Yuki Iwabuchi,
Maiko Kodama, Yu Hiasa and Ayuko Komura

1. Introduction

In the hospitality industry, sources of competitive advantage lie in employees at *gemba* who are closer to customers. Their autonomous behavior, which is consistent with strategies, enables them to serve customers with readiness and flexibility (Johnson, 1992).

Based on a qualitative survey of Toyosaki *et al.* (2018) at a hotel company A, the authors elucidate the processes of how the management control systems (MCS), constituted by budgetary control and *hoshin kanri*, leads employees' autonomous behavior to be aligned with the organizational strategy using theory of *Ba* (Itami, 2005) as the framework concept. MCS is defined as a system used by managers who want to have influence on employees so that they can behave or make decisions consistent with organizational strategies. Kikyo (2018) defines *hoshin kanri* as organizational control activities to achieve strategic goals set by an organization, which helps every employee at all levels, aligned with the goals, to respond quickly to environmental changes and to ensure continuous improvement of business performance with all-out efforts, referring to Akao (2004), Hosoya (1984), and the Japanese Society for Quality Control (2016).

However, it is difficult to remove the authors' subjectivity from the study since Toyosaki *et al.* (2018) is based on a qualitative survey. Therefore, it is necessary to make a quantitative analysis to justify their claim.

This paper attempts to verify the mechanism of MCS proposed by Toyosaki *et al.* (2018) quantitatively, using the same research site. Here, we define *Ba* (a Japanese term meaning "field") as the framework that continuously creates informative interaction among organizational members (Itami, 2005; Inoue and Suzuki, 2015).

The reason for adopting the theory of *Ba* is as follows: the theory of *Ba* explains how management tools, including MCS, generate autonomous and self-organizing behaviors of employees. The theory claims that the process in which employees come to take an action to achieve goals is a key factor to determine the outcome of management. Among a variety of management tools, MCS plays an important role in generating *Ba* since it promotes sharing issues and better understanding among organizational members (Itami and Kagono, 2003).

This paper is structured as follows: In the next section, we set hypotheses based on the theory of *Ba*. The third section describes the methodology. The fourth section presents results and discussion. In the fifth section, academic contributions of this paper and limitations that suggest future research directions are stated.

2. Hypotheses Development

2.1. *Communication in MCS and informative interaction in Ba*

As described above, *Ba* is the framework that continuously creates informative interaction among organizational members by sharing four fundamental elements of *Ba*. The four elements of *Ba* are agenda, information carrier, interpretation code, and a desire for solidarity. Agenda is typically the agenda of a meeting and is designated by what informative interaction it relates to. The designation is detailed or drafted like a type of direction. Information carrier is the method (how or where) by which employees obtain information. It could be a meeting or a report; we can even get some information based on people's expression. Interpretation code is the understanding of what the information indicates or means, for example, technical terms in operation, organizational culture, and code of behavior. Interpretation code could be different from one organization to another. A desire for solidarity is the desire to communicate or interact with others. Some people prefer to work by themselves; in that situation, their desire for solidarity is low (Itami, 2005).

The generation process of *Ba* has two steps: the first step is setting up sprouts and the second step is establishing *Ba*. Toyosaki *et al.* (2018) considers that communication by using information provided through budgetary control plays a role of preparing for sprouts of *Ba*, and that by using information provided through *hoshin kanri* plays a role of establishing *Ba*.

First, communication by using information provided through budgetary control outlines four elements of *Ba*. Based on the information, a manager shows their subordinates the direction of agenda to consider in order to achieve the budget and also provides an interpretation code which shows how to understand accounting information. Budgetary control in communication also provides information carrier, such as holding of meetings where the budget information is disseminated and discussed. Under those circumstances, a desire for solidarity will be strengthened.

Next, *hoshin kanri* driven by managers embodies and shares agenda, which are goals and measures to achieve the budget. Interpretation code in line with the measures and control items may be shared among employees if they establish the measures by themselves. Information carrier settings or meetings are also provided to disseminate *hoshin* or discuss about progress status. Bottom-up communication at those meetings enhances a desire for solidarity among participants. In this way, *hoshin kanri* propels informative interaction in *Ba*, controlling the sharing of the four elements.

Hence, communication in *hoshin kanri* can be activated by communication in budgetary control because it provides a basis for discussion of *hoshin kanri*. Communication for developing an action plan in *hoshin kanri* increases the extent of sharing the four elements, which stimulates informative interaction in *Ba*. Thus, we set the following hypotheses:

H1a: Communication in budgetary control has a positive effect on communication in *hoshin kanri*.

H1b: Communication in *hoshin kanri* has a positive effect on informative interaction in *Ba*.

2.2. *Customer orientation and informative interaction in Ba*

Informative interaction in *Ba* is enhanced since an employee in *Ba* receives external signals. External signals are the information brought from the outside of an organization such as information about external environment, information from customers or shareholders. Among various types of external information, information from customers can be the most important.

In providing interpersonal service, employees working at *gemba* who interface directly with customers must respond quickly to meet their needs. Therefore, employees must give top priority to identify not only the actualized but also the latent needs of the customer. (Kodama, 2018).

To receive the information from customers, customer-oriented organizational culture must be created. In this paper, customer-oriented organizational culture is defined as "the set of beliefs that put customers' interests first, in order to develop a long-term profitable enterprise" (Deshpandé *et al.*, 1993, p. 27).

The stronger the customer-oriented organizational culture is, the more actively employees communicate each other to satisfy customer's demand (Kohli and Jaworski, 1990; Berry, 1994; Matsuo, 2002; Wang *et al.*, 2009). From the above, we set the following hypothesis:

H2: Customer-oriented organizational culture has a positive influence on informative interaction in *Ba*.

2.3. *Conditions to stimulate informative interaction in Ba*

According to Itami (2005), organizational members need to be motivated to participate autonomously in *Ba*, which enables the management of *Ba*. In order to increase employees' motivation to join *Ba*, organizations need to satisfy basic conditions. The three conditions for this are explained in the following.

The first condition is to guarantee discretionary freedom of management. It means that organizations guarantee employees the ability to interact freely with anyone outside their group designated by the top management and have discretionary freedom of their behavior. Discretionary freedom is, in other words, empowerment. Empowerment is defined as "a doer or an organization unit which has a relatively strong authority empowers a doer or a certain organization which has no authorities" (Conger and Kanungo, 1988, p. 472). It is considered that delegating authority to employees increases their motivation to participate in *Ba* and activates informative interaction occurring there.

The second condition is to foster trust within an organization. Trust is an expectation that someone fulfills his given responsibility. In some cases, it means an expectation that someone fulfills his obligation requiring him to give priority to others' interests (Barber, 1983). Trust is effective to reduce concerns that he might behave opportunistically. Informative interaction is promoted as trust may deter concerns that he might utilize information obtained in communication with others to behave opportunistically (e.g., Davenport and Prusak, 1998; von Krogh *et al.*, 2000).

The last condition is to share basic information within an organization. Sharing basic information means that organization members share basic information including direction of organization and environmental situation through organizational mission, strategies, and so on. Dissemination of corporate mission and strategies activates dialogue and debates among employees (Simons, 1995; 2005).

Based on the discussion above, we establish three hypotheses as follows:

H3a: Freedom has a positive effect on informative interaction in *Ba*.

H3b: Trust has a positive effect on informative interaction in *Ba*.

H3c: Sharing basic information has a positive effect on informative interaction in *Ba*.

2.4. *Informative interaction in Ba and mutual understanding and psychological resonance*

Itami (2005) claimed that informative interaction in *Ba* generates mutual understanding as a consequence. Mutual understanding means that people come to share a complete picture of behavior which should be expected within the whole organization.

Itami noted that there is a micro–macro loop in the process that *Ba* influences on mutual understanding (Itami, 1999, pp. 79–82). Micro–macro loop is a virtual cycle to link micro information with macro information and to feedback and again to micro information (Imai and Kaneko, 1988, p. 80). Micro–macro loop emerges when members who participated in *Ba* share the four elements. So, Itami said that *Ba* is the framework for micro-macro loop (Itami, 1992, p. 83).Thus, we establish the following hypothesis, H4a:

H4a: Informative interaction in *Ba* has a positive effect on mutual understanding.

Informative interaction also creates psychological resonance (Itami, 2005). Psychological resonance means "sharing the same psychological state or resonant frequency arising from vibes" (Itami, 2005, p. 47). It can be interpreted as a sense of exaltation or a sense of solidarity generated in a group through good communication with colleagues in a workplace.

We use knowledge of bioholonics for basic theory. Bioholonics is a scientific research area "to study living things as information phenomena" (Shimizu and Itami, 1990, p. 28), focusing on the autonomous formation of complex ordered structure in the cells of a living organisms. In bioholonics, living things are considered as a structure of holon (including cells, and so on). Holon is defined as "an agent which has autonomous properties of self-regulating and behaving in cooperation with surrounding holons, taking the entire structure into account" (Itami, 1987, p. 60). Mutual excitation or mutual agitation is considered to occur when a holon interacts with other holons. Therefore, we establish the following hypothesis:

H4b: Informative interaction in *Ba* has a positive effect on psychological resonance.

2.5. *Mutual understanding, psychological resonance, and autonomous behavior*

Mutual understanding and psychological resonance lead employees' autonomous behavior along with organization strategies or missions (Itami, 2005). In this study, we consider autonomous behavior as kaizen activities (business improvement activities) and customer service activities. This is because the strategy of Company A, our research site, is to enhance the motivation of employees at *gemba* to improve quality of service and to help the employees listen to customers and provide services willingly in line with customer needs. Therefore, we establish the following hypotheses:

H5a: Mutual understanding has a positive effect on kaizen activities.
H5b: Mutual understanding has a positive effect on customer service activities.
H6a: Psychological resonance has a positive effect on kaizen activities.
H6b: Psychological resonance has a positive effect on customer service activities.

3. Methodology

3.1. *Research site*

The company operates about 30 luxury hotels with about 5,000 employees. The company is an industry leader in the simultaneous achievement of high customer satisfaction, low turnover rate, and high growth. The average customer satisfaction rating (using a 5-points Likert scale questionnaires) collected annually is extremely high — around 4.8 in 2016. The turnover rate for regular employees was about 9% in 2016. This is very low compared with the 28.6% average turnover rate for the hotel industry in Japan according to the Ministry of Health, Labour and Welfare Survey on Employment Trends[1] for the

---

[1]Ministry of Health, Labour and Welfare. *Survey on Employment Trends.* Available at: http://www.mhlw.go.jp/toukei/list/9-23-1.html [2017/8/2 accessed].

same year. Furthermore, the company's average annual sales growth rate between 2004 and 2016 was approximately 6%. In sum, Company A is highly regarded by both its customers and employees (Toyosaki *et al.*, 2018).

3.2. Data

Data were collected from the employees in 2016 using a questionnaire survey with a 5-points Likert scale "disagree; somewhat Disagree; I can't say either way; somewhat agree; agree" to "1 = disagree; 2 = somewhat disagree; 3 = I can't say either way; 4 = somewhat agree; 5 = agree". Targeted respondents were regular full-time employees of Company A, and the survey was conducted in November 2016 using an online questionnaire. The employees could access the questionnaire through terminal equipment at their workplace or on their own smartphones and answer questions anonymously.

The number of valid responses to the 2016 survey was 3,232. 26.1% of the responses were from employees in a managerial position and 73.9% from employees in non-managerial positions. The age distribution of the sample was as follows: Under 20 (2.7%), 20s (33.6%), 30s (22.5%), 40s (21.3%), 50s (12.3%), and 60+ (7.6%). 55.7% of the respondents were male and 44.3% were female.

3.3. Model

Figure 1 shows the model of this study.

3.4. Variables

As mentioned in the Introduction, communication in MCS plays an important role in order to generate *Ba*. Therefore, we measure the degree of communication between a manager and a subordinate in budgetary control and that in *hoshin kanri*.

- *Degree of communication in budgetary control*: To measure the degree of communication in budgetary control, we use four questions: Does

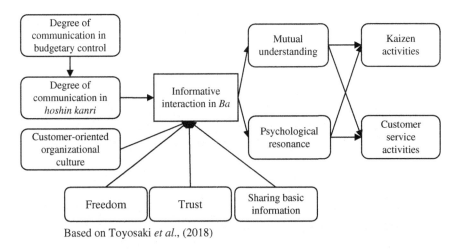

Based on Toyosaki *et al.*, (2018)

Fig. 1   Model of this study.

your boss clearly explain target figures?[2]; Do you have opportunities to discuss the target figures?; Do you have opportunities to discuss results of target figures? and Do you apply the results to the next fiscal year?

- *Degree of communication in hoshin kanri*: To measure the degree of communication in *hoshin kanri*, we use four questions: Does your boss clearly explain *hoshin*?; Do you have opportunities to discuss the targets?; Do you have opportunities to discuss the degree of achieving the *hoshin*? and Do you apply the results to the next fiscal year?

- *Customer-oriented organizational culture*: Customer-oriented organizational culture is measured with four questions inquiring whether or not employees have a norm of placing importance on fulfilling customer needs and feel satisfaction in achieving it. These measurements were developed by Brown *et al.* (2002), and we changed them to plain language so that employees of Company A could easily understand.

- *Freedom*: Freedom is measured with two questions inquiring about the extent of freedom to make decisions at work at their own discretion.

---

[2]Employees at *gemba* are less familiar with the term, "budget". We discussed it with personnel of Company A in charge of the survey and decided to use "target figures" instead (Toyosaki, 2018).

- *Trust*: Trust is measured with a total of five questions inquiring about the level of trust which subordinates have toward managers and the trust relationship among subordinates.
- *Sharing basic information*: Sharing basic information is measured with a total of four questions inquiring about the understanding of strategies, the level of acquisition of necessary information and knowledge to pursue their roles, and the level of sympathy toward the corporate mission.
- *Informative interaction in Ba*: informative interaction in *Ba* is measured with two questions inquiring if customer needs and information are shared among members of a department and how many issues and solutions are shared among them.
- *Mutual understanding*: Mutual understanding is measured with three questions inquiring if members of a department understand their respective roles relative to each other, if they know what to do in case of any task assigned to them, and if roles are clearly assigned among them.
- *Psychological resonance*: Psychological resonance is measured by two questions inquiring if there exists energy in a department where a respondent works and if a respondent inspires his colleagues to cooperate and work with one another.
- *Kaizen activities*: Kaizen activities are measured with two questions inquiring if employees are willing to addressing improvement of business within a department and if there exists a climate of improving business there.
- *Customer service activities*: Customer service activities are measured with two questions inquiring if they listen to customer claims and if they deal with such claims in cooperation with other employees within a department. At Company A, the term "claims" covers a broad range of meanings. They are not limited to customer claims but include requests and demand from customers. Company A refers to them collectively as "customer claim".
- *Control Variables*: We selected control variables for informative interaction as follows: Position (manager = 1, non-manager = 0), Gender (male = 1, female = 0), Hotel rating (S or superior = 1, others = 0), (A or good = 1, others = 0), and length of employment (1st year = 1, others = 0), (2nd

year = 1, others = 0), (3rd year = 1, others = 0), (4th–5th years = 1, others = 0), (6th–10th years = 1, others = 0), (11th–15th years = 1, others = 0).

Table 1 shows each item of average point and standardized deviation (S.D.), which was employed for confirmatory factor analysis.

3.5. *Confirmatory factor analysis*

First, we conducted a confirmatory factor analysis using maximum likelihood method (Anderson and Gerbing, 1988; Bollen, 1989) to determine whether or not the item indicators of the degree of communication in budgetary control, the degree of communication in *hoshin kanri*, customer-oriented organizational culture, freedom, trust, sharing basic information, informative interaction, mutual understanding, psychological resonance, kaizen activities, and customer service activities demonstrated adequate loadings on the latent variables and to test the overall fit of the measurement model.

The test of the measurement model revealed good loadings for the indicators on the latent variables, and the overall model had a good fit, χ^2 = 10587.826, df = 748, GFI = 0.856, AGFI = 0.792, CFI = 0.901, RMSEA = 0.064. The closer the GFI is to 1, the better, corresponding to the coefficient of determination in a multiple regression analysis (the degree to which the total variance of the saturated model can explain the variance of the estimated model). The GFI for the model is 0.856, indicating that it is a model with a high degree of explanatory power. AGFI corresponds to the coefficient of determination adjusted for the degrees of freedom in a multiple regression analysis. The AGFI for the model is 0.792, indicating that there is no problem with its explanatory power. As the CFI was bigger than 0.7 and RMSEA is good, at 0.064, the model is used.

4. Results and Discussion

Path analysis by covariance structure analysis using maximum likelihood method is conducted to consider the validity of the model. Goodness of fit index is as follows: χ^2 = 12967.191, df = 841, GFI = 0.830, AGFI = 0.781,

Table 1. Descriptive statistic.

Variable	Questions	Mean	S.D.
Degree of communication in budgetary control	Does your boss clearly explain target figures?	4.22	0.92
	Do you have opportunities to discuss the target figures?	4.01	1.06
	Do you have opportunities to discuss results of target figures?	3.75	1.11
	Do you apply the result to the next fiscal year?	3.74	1.06
Degree of communication in *hoshin kanri*	Does your boss clearly explain *hoshin*?	4.01	1.03
	Do you have opportunities to discuss the targets?	3.87	1.09
	Do you have opportunities to discuss the degree of achieving the *hoshin*?	3.92	1.04
	Do you apply the result to the next fiscal year?	3.90	1.02
Customer-oriented organizational culture	Are you trying to understand the customers in order to know their needs?	4.60	0.64
	Do you feel satisfied to respond promptly to customer's request?	4.52	0.67
	Do you think that satisfying customers (or internal customers) is more important than anything else?	4.54	0.68
	Are you actively make efforts to know the individual personality of each customer?	4.36	0.81
Freedom	Do you have the freedom to deal with your work based on your own judgement?	4.08	0.91
	Do you have some extent of discretionary freedom in your work?	4.13	0.91
Trust	Is the direction of your direct manager understandable?	4.21	0.99
	Does your direct manager take responsibility of your activities?	4.38	0.93
	Are departmental members acting on behalf of the entire department?	4.00	0.98

	Do department members sometimes help you by postponing their work as needed?	4.12	0.98
	Do you feel the relationship of trust between the members of the department is strong?	3.95	1.03
Sharing basic information	Do you read every issue of the buletin at work?	4.61	0.63
	Do you gain necessary information from XX (information system of Company A)?	3.57	1.33
	Do you gain necessary knowledge from e learning?	3.25	1.29
	Are you able to explain "YY" (Medium-Term Business Plan of Company A)?	4.51	0.73
	Are you able to sympathize with the corporate mission?	3.30	1.17
Informative interaction in *Ba*	Do you always share issues or solutions with your colleagues?	4.25	0.83
	Do you always share the updated customer needs and new information given by customers with your colleagues in the department?	4.29	0.80
Mutual understanding	Do you know what to do with each other?	4.16	0.86
	Do you know who is doing what job in your department?	4.37	0.78
	Are the tasks shared appropriately?	4.21	0.90
Psychological resonance	Do you feel a sense of value and fulfilment in your current job?	3.95	1.08
	In your current job, are there times when you are so absorbed in your work that time flies?	3.89	1.17
Kaizen activities	Are you carefully listening to complaints from customers?	4.61	0.63
	When claims arise, do you coordinate to solve them in the department?	4.57	0.68
Customer service activities	Are you discussing ideas about business improvement?	4.02	0.92
	Does your department have a climate to accept proposals for business improvement?	4.14	0.95

CFI = 0.878, RMSEA = 0.067. The overall model has a good fit. Therefore, the model is adopted.

We also find that control variables have a positive and significant influence on the informative interaction in *Ba*: Position (0.022, $p < 0.05$) and hotel rating S (0.051, $p < 0.001$) and A (0.038, $p < 0.05$). It shows that managers tend to have more informative interaction in a workplace than other employees. In addition, the higher the hotels are rated, the more sophisticated quality of service they are expected to offer. Therefore, it is considered that employees need to cooperate with each other, which increases informative interaction.

Figure 2 demonstrates the results of the analysis of covariance structure. First, the result clarified that the degree of communication in budgetary control has a significant positive influence (0.896, $p < 0.001$) on the degree of communication in *hoshin kanri*, which supported H1a.

It also revealed that the degree of communication in *hoshin kanri* has a significant positive influence (0.276, $p < 0.001$) on informative interaction generated in *Ba*, which supported H1b. The results above may be interpreted to mean that the degree of communication through MCS generates *Ba* by the sharing of the four elements of *Ba* and activates informative interaction occurring in *Ba*.

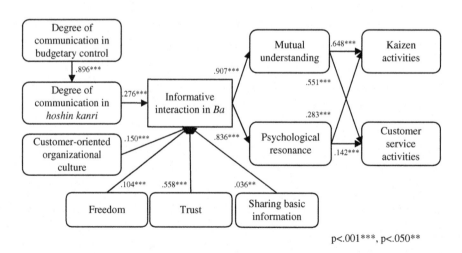

p<.001***, p<.050**

Fig. 2   The results of the analysis.

Second, customer-oriented organizational culture which increases willingness to receive customer information has a significant positive effect on informative interaction in *Ba*, which supported H2. It is considered that the results are consistent with previous studies (Kohli and Jaworski, 1990; Berry, 1994; Matsuo, 2002; Wang *et al.*, 2009). That is, customer-oriented organizational culture enhances communication among members.

Third, it was found that all of the three variables considered to enhance a desire to participate in *Ba* have significant positive influences on informative interaction occurring in *Ba*: trust (0.558, $p < 0.001$), freedom (0.104, $p < 0.001$), and sharing basic information (0.036, $p < 0.001$). The findings supported H3a, H3b, and H3c. They also supported Itami (2005)'s claim consequently.

The combined influence of those three variables and customer-oriented organizational culture on informative interaction is 0.848 in total, more influential than the 0.523 which is the total of the indirect effect of the degree of communication in budgetary control on informative interaction (0.247) and the direct effect of the degree of communication in *hoshin kanri* on informative interaction (0.276). It shows that the effect brought about by informative interaction might be limited without customer-oriented organizational culture, freedom, trust, and sharing basic information, even if the degree of communication in MCS is highly enhanced. In particular, the most influential variable on informative interaction is Trust. Trust is indispensable above all to generate self-organizing behavior through informative interaction.

Fourth, it reveals that informative interaction occurring in *Ba* has a significant positive influence on mutual understanding (0.907, $p < 0.001$), which supports H4a. It demonstrates that mutual understanding of each other's responsibilities is formed among employees in a department who aim to achieve the given objectives.

It is also clear that informative interaction occurring in *Ba* has a significant positive influence (0.836, $p < 0.001$) on psychological resonance, which supported H4b. It is interpreted that a sense of exaltation will be nurtured by mutual excitation generated with the surrounding people during informative interaction.

Fifth, mutual understanding sharing is demonstrated to have a significant positive influence on kaizen activities (0.648, $p < 0.001$) and customer service activities (0.551, $p < 0.001$), and thus H5a and H5b are supported.

Psychological resonance is shown to have a significant positive influence on kaizen activities (0.283, $p < 0.001$) and customer service activities (0.142, $p < 0.001$), and thus H6a and H6b are supported. It is considered that psychological resonance generated in communication with the surrounding people through informative interaction might become a form of psychological energy which allows people to behave autonomously.

In summary, first, creation of employees' autonomous and self-organizing behavior begins with preparation of basic conditions, which motivates employees to participate in *Ba*. Next, communication through MCS generates *Ba*, and employees who have willingness to collect and disseminate customer information under customer-oriented organizational culture activate informative interaction in *Ba*. Then, informative interaction in *Ba* helps employees to have a common image of the necessary actions that need to be taken and helps systematize their responsibilities, or who should do what. In parallel, a sense of exaltation is generated among employees, leading to the development of circumstances which promote autonomous and self-organizing behavior of employees.

5. Conclusion

The purpose of this study is to verify the mechanism of MCS proposed by Toyosaki *et al.* (2018) quantitatively, using a questionnaire survey conducted at Company A, a hotel company.

The results support Toyosaki *et al.* (2018)'s theoretical framework. Precisely, customer-oriented organizational culture and basic conditions increase employees' motivation to join *Ba*, which creates informative interaction with a high degree of communication in MCS. This informative interaction fosters mutual understanding and psychological resonance among employees and motivates them to behave autonomously.

5.1. *Contribution*

First, it can be an MCS model launched in Japan which enables bottom-up empowerment (Johnson, 1992), not the traditional top-down control.

The MCS model used here incorporates *hoshin kanri*, an MCS originated in Japan, and is designed to activate free and closer informative interaction among employees. Against such a background, it establishes the order of responsibilities in a self-organizing way and generates mutual excitation, which motivates employees to implement autonomous behavior, self-organizing behavior, and learning.

Second, it made a contribution to the management control package (MCP, Malmi and Brown, 2008). This paper gives insight on the influence of freedom, trust, sharing basic information, and customer-oriented organizational culture on informative interaction which is promoted by communication through MCS. Freedom corresponds to administrative control (Malmi and Brown, 2008), trust to social control (Dekker, 2004), and basic information sharing and customer-oriented organizational culture to cultural control or planning control (Malmi and Brown, 2008). Our model, introducing those elements, contributes to MCP in which MCS functions by getting other control systems involved as well.

5.2. *Future research*

We suggest three ideas for future research.

(1) Building a higher level concept of management control which may function with our MCS model. Our model is self-organizing but does not always do so in line with the strategies and direction shown by the top management. Itami (2005), the advocator of the theory of *Ba*, describes that motivation of participation and functions of *Ba* depends on how a manager of *Ba* controls multiple *Ba* toward strategic goals. To verify his idea, we need to create a place or *Ba* and align its direction with the corporate mission. In some cases, we need a control to eliminate and consolidate *Ba*.

(2) Clarifying mutual relationship among communication through MCS, freedom (administrative control), trust (social control), sharing basic information (cultural control and planning control), and customer-oriented organizational culture (cultural control). MCP theory states that MCS works together with other control systems. Solving issues concerning common bias. The survey we use here is limited to a

questionnaire survey on employees. We must admit that it contains a problem of common bias. To solve this problem, we need to incorporate dependent variables such as the number of kaizen (improvement) proposals by employees, new service proposals, customer satisfaction index, and financial performance into our analysis model.

(3) Necessity to expand research center/unit or research sites. This paper is only an empirical/case study done by surveying just one hotel company, Company A. We need to analyze the survey result by classifying the data into business categories or job categories. The classification will be useful to clarify differences created in the process to promote autonomous behavior. To pursue future research, we need to explore, review, and secure research sites at other hotel companies or in other business categories.

References

Akao, Y. 2004. *Hoshin Kanri: Policy Deployment for Successful TQM*, New York, NY: Productivity Press.

Anderson, J. C. and Gerbing, D. W. 1988. Structural equation modeling in practice: A review and recommended two-step approach. *Psychological Bulletin*, 103(3), 411–423.

Barber, B. 1983. *The Logic and Limits of Trust*, New York, NY: Basic Books.

Berry, L. 1994. The employee as customers, *Journal of Retail Banking*, 3, 25–80.

Bollen, K. A. 1989. A new incremental fit index for general structural equation models, *Sociological Methods & Research*, 17(3), 303–316.

Brown, T. J., Mowen, J. C., Donavan, D. T., and Licata. J. W. 2002. The Customer Orientation of Service Workers: Personality Trait Determinants and Effects on Self- and Supervisor Performance Ratings, *Journal of Marketing Research*, 39, 110–119.

Conger, J. A. and Kanungo, R. N. 1988. The empowerment process: Integrating theory and practice, *Academy of management review*, 13(3), 471–482.

Davenport, T. H. and Prusak, L. 1998. *Working knowledge: How Organizations Manage What they Know*, Boston, MA: Harvard Business School Press.

Dekker, H. C. 2004. Control of Inter-Organizational Relationships: Evidence on Appropriation Concerns and Coordination Requirements, *Accounting, Organizations and Society*, 29(1), 27–49.

Deshpandé, R., Farley, J. U., and Webster Jr, F. E. 1993. Corporate culture, customer orientation, and innovativeness in Japanese firms: A quadrad analysis. *The Journal of Marketing*, 57(1), 23-37.

Hosoya, K. 1984. *How to View and Think about Things like QC,* Tokyo: JUSE Press (in Japanese).

Inoue. K. and Suzuki. K. 2015. How has "Management of *Ba*" been developed?: Itami's research from Management control systems to Management of Ba, *Colombo Business Journal*, 5(2) and 6(1), 42–54.

Itami, H. 1987. Informational interaction and management, In Imai, K. (eds), *TheEcology of Economics*, Tokyo: NTT Publications (in Japanese).

Itami, H. 1992. The Firm as an Informational *"Ba"* (Interactive Field), In Ijiri, Y. and Nakano, I. (eds.), *Information and Internationalization of Firms*, Pittsburgh, PA: Carnegie-Mellon University Press.

Itami, H. 1999. *"Ba" Management*, Tokyo: NTT Publications (in Japanese).

Itami, H. 2005. *Theory of "Ba" and Management*, Tokyo: Toyo Keizai Shinpo, (in Japanese).

Itami, H. and Kagono, T. 2003. *Seminar Introduction to Management*, Tokyo: Nikkei Inc. (in Japanese).

Imai, K. and Kaneko, I. 1988. *Network Organization Theory*, Tokyo: Iwanami Shoten, (in Japanese).

Johnson, H. T. 1992. *Relevance Regained: From Top-Down Control to Bottom-Up Empowerment*, New York, NY: The Free Press.

JSQC-Std 33-001. 2016. *Hoshin kanri Guidelines*, Japanese Society for Quality Control (in Japanese).

Kikyo, M. 2018. Synergy between budgetary control and hoshin management: Empirical analysis using questionnaire survey in a hotel company, *Japanese Journal of Strategic Management*. accepted. (in Japanese).

Kodama, M. 2018. Validity of the conceptual framework of management control process based on construction concept of the Ba theory — Analysis based on questionnaire survey at hotel company A —, *Japanese Journal of Strategic Management*, 6(2), 81–99 (in Japanese).

Kohli, A. K. and Jaworski, B. J. 1990. Market orientation: The construct, research proposition, and managerial implications, *Journal of Marketing*, 54(2), 1–18.

Malmi, T. and Brown, D. A. 2008. Management control systems as a package — Opportunities, challenges and research directions, *Management Accounting Research*, 19(4), 287–300.

Matsuo, M. 2002. Innovation of sales organization, *Journal of Marketing and Distribution*, 5, 61–78.

Ministry of Health, Labor and Welfare. 2016. Survey on Labor Employment Trend. http://www.mhlw.go.jp/toukei/list/9-23-1.html (dated: 2017.08.02) (in Japanese).

Shimizu, H. and Itami, H. 1990. Firm as Informational Nexus, In: Itami, H., *Management File '90*, Tokyo: Chikuma-shobo (in Japanese).

Simons, R. 1995. *Levers of Control: How Managers Use Innovative Control Systems to Drive Strategic Renewal*, Boston, MA: Harvard Business School Press.

Simons, R. 2005. *Levers of Organization Design: How Managers Use Accountability Systems for Great Performance and Commitment*, Boston, MA: Harvard Business School Press.

Toyosaki, H., Kodama, M., Kikyo, M. and Suzuki, K. 2018. Management control systems for motivating employees' goal congruent and autonomous behaviour: Conceptual framework based on qualitative research and Ba theory, *Japanese Journal of Strategic Management*, 6(2), 37–60 (in Japanese).

Toyosaki, H. 2018. Management Control Systems for Facilitating Horizontal Communication: Integrating Hierarchy and Autonomy, *Journal of Strategic Management*, 6(2), 61–80 (in Japanese).

von Krogh, G., Ichijo, K. and Nonaka, I. 2000. *Enabling Knowledge Creation: How to Unlock the Mystery of Tacit Knowledge and Release the Power of Innovation*, New York, NY: Oxford University Press.

Wang, C., Hult, M., Ketchen, J., and Ahmed, P. 2009. Knowledge management orientation, market orientation and firm performance: An integration and empirical examination, *Journal of Strategic Marketing*, 17, 99–122.

Index

Printed in the United States
By Bookmasters